To En

C000193309

You too can be an expert
in everything!

best wishes,

Ken

THE JOY OF KEV

What they said* about The Joy of Kev:

'I'm now striding through death with a new found confidence. Thanks, Kev.' - Plato

'The Joy of Kev. No toilet should be without it.' - Thomas Crapper

'Please tell me we're not paying this fool.' - Editor, *Oldham Evening Chronicle*

'He's not the new messiah, he's a very silly boy.' - Kevin's Mother

* allegedly

THE JOY OF KEV

An indispensible guide to modern living

Kevin Fitzpatrick

Scratching Shed Publishing Ltd

First published by Scratching Shed Publishing Ltd in 2010
Registered in England & Wales No. 6588772.
Registered office:
47 Street Lane, Leeds, West Yorkshire. LS8 1AP

www.scratchingshedpublishing.co.uk

ISBN 978-0956478719

All photographs © Kevin Fitpatrick

A catalogue record for this book is available from the British
Library.

Typeset in Warnock Pro Semi Bold, Lucida Calligraphy
and Palatino

Printed and bound in the United Kingdom by
CPI Antony Rowe, Chippenham, Wiltshire

For my wife Victoria, Ruby, Luke and Bump

'Bikkies es vilis pro dipping'

The Contents of Kev

As you wander along the road of life it's likely that every now and then you'll have days when you think, 'I didn't have garlic last night, did I?' It's at moments like this, when you're baffled and in need of some chewing gum, that one of these carefully chosen subject titles may help.

Kev's continued contents

The Acknowledgements of Kev

T here are lots of people to thank for their contribution to this book.

Firstly, my parents, who, despite bringing me up on an ordinary street in Oldham, somehow managed to raise a child with delusions of grandeur.

My dear departed grandad Niel Christopher - whose quotes throughout these pages are genuine and who taught me that a good piece of advice will last a lifetime.

Jim Williams, former editor of the *Oldham Evening Chronicle*, who agreed to print my articles under the header of 'Learn with Kev'; and everyone who approached me in the street and said, 'I've seen that rubbish you keep putting in the paper. It's alright actually.' My mate Bri, a loyal fan from the start.

Thanks too to my cousin Misha for suggesting that I set up the Facebook group and to everyone who joined and then invited their friends to do so. To Tony and Phil at Scratching Shed, who realised that the world was in need of a new spiritual leader and that I'd do until one appeared.

Nor must I forget my sister, Hannah, who would kill me if she didn't get a mention. Or my babies, Ruby and Luke - the inspiration for so many amusing stories you couldn't make up - for the joy they give me every single day.

And finally, thank you to my wife Victoria, for loving me, humouring me and guiding me back down to earth whenever I get too carried away.

✳

The Joy of Being Wise

I was standing in the park wondering why frisbees get bigger as they get closer. Then it hit me.

I held one hand up and pointed my forefinger to the sky as I looked around for someone who could share in the wisdom of my great discovery. A spotty kid asked for his Frisbee back. He'll do, I thought.

'I think I exist, therefore I exist, I think!' I exclaimed. 'Just give me the frisbee,' he said. 'Yes, my son,' I replied, trying to nod with a reassuring worldliness. 'What you on about, loser?' he said. I decided it was time I invested in a bigger white beard.

I sat under a tree and pondered another of life's great questions, that one about gravity. All of a sudden an apple hit me on the head. It was that flippin' spotty teenager again. I had a bite and threw it back.

Another question fell from my lips. 'If a man stands alone in a forest and says something outside the earshot of any living thing, is he still wrong?' A woman walking a dog shouted, 'Yes.'

The Joy of Being Wise

Being accepted as wise, I was finding, wasn't quite as easy as I'd hoped. But I knew I had knowledge and advice which could benefit others. Good advice. Advice that had been passed down from generation to generation and never been used.

Things like… when in doubt, worry. Love your enemies, it'll confuse them. Cast bread upon the waters, but make sure the tide's coming in. If you've got to work for an idiot, you may as well work for yourself.

In centuries gone by, if you were wise I'm guessing you just stood on a big rock and an audience would gather around you. These days, though, we're in competition with the telly and those upon it. Modern day philosophers like Trisha and Jeremy Kyle. I'm not sure who shouted at young people on benefits in the olden days, but they can't have done it with as much style as Jezza.

By now it was raining and my beard was coming unstuck. I decided to give up being wise and wait until I was a grandparent like everyone else.

My grandad, after all, was the wisest person I knew. He made it look easy. He'd say: 'An hour before midnight's worth two in the morning.' 'You should only itch your eye with your elbow' (that's impossible, by the way). And his favourite: 'Make sure you cut that hedge straight. People will think I've done it.'

I was only twelve, so I had plenty of time really. All the time in the world, someone wise might say. And then they'd probably repeat the last bit for added affect. All the time in the world.

*

The Joy of Breathing

I f you don't know how to do this already then you're
in trouble, because breathing is the basis for human
life. It's the process which takes air and, importantly, oxygen
into the body and spits the carbon dioxide back out.

Your first and last breaths will be your most significant.
The first will have been a joyous moment for your parents,
who undoubtedly looked on adoringly, not quite believing
they could be responsible for the creation of a tiny being of
such magnificence and beauty.

Your last breath is likely to be a much more sombre affair
but, with a bit of luck, you'll be able to go with a gentle
wheeze as you cock your hat to a life well lived.

In the intervening years I'm guessing you'll have done
lots of breathing and, hopefully, some of it will have been
heavy. And not just down a phone to a stranger you've cold-
called when drunk.

Women are quite keen that any potential lover should
take their breath away. It's on the tick list alongside 'must
love me just the way I am' and 'must allow me to change

The Joy of Breathing

him'. Taking my first tentative steps into seduction, I soon realised that accidently winding them didn't count.

Our innate desire to procreate means the regularity of breathing will happily be sacrificed to make oneself more attractive. Ladies won't breathe all evening if it means they can fit into their chosen dress. Men, always the lazier half of the species, prefer to breathe in only when potential partners walk past if they have a physique they'd like to hide. It's actually a bit of a disaster if the object of their desire stops to talk and their gut has to be unleashed after two minutes of silent nodding.

A big, deep breath is considered the remedy for many an affliction and it's especially useful if you've had a bit of a shock. Perhaps you've found that credit card bill your partner hid under the fridge. All you need is some nice, deep breaths. Take in some air and calm yourself down. Then follow it up with a nice cup of tea. A. Nice. Cup. Of. Tea.

Generally, other people will be quite supportive of your need to continue breathing unless you exhale the kind of eye-watering tang that makes passing sparrows fall from the sky. An immediate remedy is to gaffer tape your mouth and breathe through your nose. Alternatively, I'd recommend cleaning your teeth occasionally and avoiding a combination of black coffee, cigarettes and garlic bread at breakfast.

The Joy of Sleeping

aving a nap. Catching some zzzzzs. Treating yourself to a snooze. Going to bed early, getting up late. Snuggling up. Having a bit of shut-eye. All these are variations of sleep and what a wonderful bedfellow it is.

Sleep is a naturally recurring state of relatively suspended sensory and motor activity, characterised by total or partial unconsciousness and the inactivity of nearly all voluntary muscles. Strange, then, that women think men are totally responsible for the fact that they snore.

The average adult needs seven or eight hours kip a day. For young children, it's crucial to their development. You grow when you're asleep. But it's only when they become teenagers that they start to demand 17 hours a day on a weekend.

Some people pride themselves on being able to sleep anywhere. 'I sleep like a log, me,' they say, as if having a disdain for comfort is a talent. My Dad's well known for it. He once got up to see to a crying baby in the night and, a few minutes later, my Mum had to get up aswell and climb over him as he slept on the nursery floor.

The Joy of Sleeping

Falling asleep in public can be embarrassing, especially if the sambucas were your idea. Once well drunk, you're not too fussy about where you lay your hat. Night club dance floors, park benches and even inappropriate people's beds will do.

Waking up tends to be the real problem if you're asleep in public though. There are few things more excruciating than coming round with a snort on a packed train. Perhaps the next moment when the stranger sitting opposite suggests you wipe the dribble from your chin is one of them.

Sleeping with the enemy can be a risky business, but I suppose that's what married life is all about. If, when you open your eyes in a morning, you can gaze adoringly at the snoring lump beside you, you're set up for life.

And if you've not had any sleep for a while you'll certainly know about it. When your body decides it can stay awake no longer you yawn like a hippopotamus, one eye begins to twitch and you desperately raise your eyebrows and attempt to lift your eyelids. But it's to no avail. Within seconds you know you'll be gone and you are. Then the lights change and people behind you start beeping.

The final word goes to those poor souls who can't get any sleep. It's no wonder you've got insomnia if you just lie there awake all night is it? I'd suggest you try sleeping right on the edge of the bed. With a bit of luck you'll drop off in no time.

*

The Joy of Being in Love

A h, love… it's like a summers day, warm and uplifting. It's an irresistible glimpse of heaven, a friendship set on fire. It's like hot chocolate, sweet, tasty and bit sickly. It's like war, easy to begin but hard to end.

You'll know you're in love by the intense affection and fondness you feel for the object of your desire. Your knees will be weak and your puppy dog eyes will suggest to everyone you stumble into that you've been hit by Cupid's arrow.

Most people have their first taste of love as a teenager and it usually leaves them feeling nauseous. Girls tend to fall in love with older boys and popstars, while boys fall for girls who are in love with older boys and popstars. As you mature you should learn to accept your limits a bit more.

When the stalking eventually pays off and a love is finally reciprocated, it has to be said it's pretty fantastic. All of a sudden you understand why lovers skip across fields to reach each other. You realise that love can conquer all and that anything is possible with this amazing person by your

The Joy of Being in Love

side. Then they dump you and not even the promise of your Mum's best Spanish omelette can bring you around.

As Rod Stewart points out, the first cut is the deepest, but you should get back on that horse. There are plenty more fish in the sea. It's better to have loved and lost then never to have loved at all, etc etc. Plus, as your Dad says, she'll be a big 'un when she's older.

Finding a love that lasts can be quite a challenge in the modern world because there's so much choice and everyone has such high expectations. It's not as simple as it was in the olden days when you just married your cousin.

Ideally, you're looking for someone you fancy who makes you laugh, who'll love you for being you and won't try to stop you seeing your friends.

A good place to start the search is uptown on a Friday night with the look of love in your eyes. The more you drink, the more desperate that look will become and the less fussy you'll be. If no-one is falling for you, it may be that you have to start tripping people up. You can also try the internet but, be warned, that model with a lovely personality you've found may have a moustache and only be after a passport.

With a bit of luck and after trying on a few duffers, you'll find the love of your life and unbridled happiness can reign. The next logical step is to get married.

You can't go on enjoying yourself forever.

*

The Joy of Dance

In my view, there are three kinds of dancers. There are those who were born to do it, those who have to work at it and some who really shouldn't bother. I like to consider myself a combination of all three.

I've found that being a great dancer comes with responsibility. Sometimes I don't feel like spinning for the third time, but I do because the joy I see in people's faces softens the pain of my stitch.

It might be hard to believe, but I've not always been the Lord of the Dance. In fact, many years ago, a woman came up to me at a party and said: 'You're not a very good dancer.' I said: 'Dancing? I'm just trying to stay on my feet.' But I always knew it took a lot of rhythm to miss every single beat, so there was hope. And things were about to change dramatically.

I began to study what I soon realised was an art and, before long, was throwing out moves on the dance floor like they were going out of fashion. In truth, many of them already had.

The Joy of Dance

As the months and years went by I continued to add to my repertoire. The foxtrot, the moonwalk and the waltz... I couldn't do any of those, but I had picked up the barn dance and the Can Can.

My rule of thumb is try any move once, twice if you've built up a enough momentum. Hip hop, a ya don't stop the rock. Twist and shout, break those bad beats and remember, guilty feet ain't got no rhythm.

Unfortunately, for a dance god, jealousy can lead to wild accusations. I'm often accused of having had dancing lessons. People say it's impossible to achieve what I do with charisma alone. And it doesn't stop there. I was once accused of running a dictatorship on a night out when someone claimed that I 'ruled' the nightclub we were in. Ridiculously, on another night it was suggested I'd taken the dance floor out with me. I denied it of course, but people wouldn't stop saying that I 'owned' it.

So, close your eyes and dance like nobody's watching but be aware that they probably will be, especially if you keep banging into people. And finally, a couple of warnings. If you're a young pup, don't try too hard, nobody likes a sweaty dancer. If you're getting on a bit, be aware of the risk of dislocation.

The Joy of Being Fashionable

I had a final look in the mirror as I headed out the door, braced for admiring glances. With a chequered flat cap on backwards and a leather jacket with an eagle on the back, I knew I was pushing the fashion boundaries, but I hadn't expected the outfit to still get mentioned years later amid fits of giggles.

'Do you remember when he came out in that spread eagle jacket?' my friends still remember with nauseating fondness. 'What a geek.'

Then there were those white jeans I borrowed off my brother. They were a bit too tight but surely no-one would notice. They did. And when they're laughing about the jacket, I know my friends are only moments away from recalling the time I wore 'my mum's white jeans'.

I don't think of them as fashion disasters, more as brave attempts to lead the way. I'm a slave to the style, and pride myself on anticipating the latest trends. Stripy things, things with buttons, clogs... I was there from the start with all three. Although I must admit that even I didn't predict that trend

The Joy of Being Fashionable

where things were supposed to 'match'. Overnight, my entire wardrobe was obsolete.

If you are going to be fashionable then individuality isn't really achievable. You need to wear what everyone else is wearing and make sure it's the young and chic and not the recently retired. Like a fashion conscious sheep, you've got to graze while modelling the latest craze. In this dress you're in. In that dress you're popping out. Your trousers are up. My pants are down.

As a general rule, fashions do come round again, much like the vegetable Chinese dish on the Lazy Susan, but my personal fashion favourite of all time may have gone forever. Everyone had a shell suit in the early nineties, literally everyone. Whole families wore them. Couples swished hand in hand in their matching purple suits with luminous green flashes. You don't get tracksuits like that anymore, which is why it's lucky I've kept all mine.

Being at the forefront of fashion can be a risky business, but my motto is: If you feel good, you're probably looking good. Just don't be offended when people say: 'What have you come as?'

*

The Joy of Being Polite

I f manners maketh the man, there's work to be done with our youngest.

He recently burped before announcing: 'I burp!' My wife said: 'No, what do you say?' And he replied: 'Ahhhhhh, buuurrrpp!' as he lifted his arms in celebration.

Instilling manners and politeness in a child is one of a parent's main jobs, alongside making them eat vegetables and teaching them to play blackjack. It's a challenge because there really is no calling for politeness in the animal kingdom and that, after all, is where we are originally from.

By all means take time out to deal with 'drawing on the wall' and 'weeing in the kitchen cupboard'. But what needs serious pressure and most concentration from you is the mission to get your politeness project to say please, thank you and excuse me. These are the words your offspring's future mother-in-law will be listening out for the first time she meets them.

Once they're on board with the pleasantries of exchanging objects, they can move onto apologies for bodily

The Joy of Being Polite

functions which, while appearing fun, are actually considered uncouth. Politeness should become automatic, so after a while there should be no need for raised eyebrows or crossed arms to beckon out a begrudging, 'peees.'

Those who happen to enjoy talking with their mouth full and pushing into queues may question what all the fuss is about. Why, they may also wonder, can't the English tell a woman that she's got her dress tucked in her knickers as she walks down the high street? Because that would be rude and common courtesy costs nothing.

If you want to be polite you should avoid saying awkward or inappropriate things to people you don't know. Asking strangers questions like: 'So why did she leave you?' or 'Do you want me to finish that chop?' are certainly not good etiquette, although it's never stopped my Dad.

But the rules of politeness do vary around the world. In China, for example, their concept of personal body space is very different to ours. It's not considered impolite to spit or stare. In England, you're not even supposed to stare if someone sits on your knee on a bus and begins spitting.

You do have to move with the times though because, like everything else, politeness continues to evolve. Apparently, on a night on the town, it's now no longer the done thing to open a door for a lady. It's actually more polite to carry them through it and hold them up until their friends arrive. If you've been out recently, you probably already know about that one.

*

The Joy of Being Musical

Ask most people for their one regret in life and there's a good chance they'll say it's never having learnt to play a musical instrument. Sadly, I too am in that rueful group, but not through lack of trying.

One of my earliest memories is of banging a pan with a spoon on the kitchen floor. The song says that the rhythm is gonna get you, but for some reason it didn't get me. The recorder followed at primary school; three blind mice being a particular favourite although admittedly quite a challenge.

I attempted the piano next. Plonkity plonk. Plank. Plonk. There were some beautiful moments, but some terrible quarters of an hour. I answered a knock at the front door and a man said: 'Hello, I'm the piano tuner.' I said: 'I haven't ordered one.' He said: 'No, but your neighbour did.'

Undeterred, I decided to join a band, because if you're going to attract the opposite sex, it really helps if you're a rock star.

The only one that would have me was a brass band and I found it's not that easy to wink at potential groupies if

The Joy of Being Musical

you're marching, cheeks puffed, in the shadow of an overweight trombone player.

I asked one female fan if she wanted to make sweet music. She said I could whistle for it. I had to admit that I probably couldn't.

I'd hoped my music was better than it sounded but I eventually had to concede it wasn't working for anyone's ears. Nevertheless, I still have some tips for you. If you want to be musical you've got to hit the right notes in the order right and timing is.

Everything. It does help if you know a bit of musical parlance... 1. A flat minor is when you drop a piano down a mine shaft. 2. A flat major is if you drop a piano on an army base. 3. Chords are trousers worn by librarians. 4. The English horn is neither English nor a horn and not to be confused with the French horn, which is German.

If you can't play an instrument then you can share the gift of song but not everyone's share is equal. The best places are in the shower, while waiting at traffic lights, or on the *X Factor* in front of millions of people, especially if you're rubbish.

Be warned though, being musical isn't generally a fast track to fame and fortune. If two people are walking down the street and one of them is a musician, there's a good chance the other one will be unemployed as well.

Having said that, there's a busker in Liverpool who just pretends to play Beatles songs on a cardboard cut-out of a guitar and he makes an absolute fortune. People tip him for his cheek. It makes you wish you'd learnt to play one of those at school doesn't it?

*

The Joy of Ordering the Usual

W hen you order the usual and receive the confirmation of a nod and a knowing smile, it creates a warm sense of belonging. You can wink at other people in the queue to indicate that you go there all the time and they absolutely definitely recognise you. But used inappropriately, or in the wrong company, ordering the usual can be a frustrating and lonely business, as I've found out the hard way.

A friend and I used to go to the same cafe every day and order the same thing. After a couple of months we'd walk there saying: 'He has got to ask us if it's the usual today!' He'd say: 'What can I get you lads?' We'd reply: 'The usual please!' And with a puzzled look he'd ask: 'So what's that then?' We were hurt and humiliated. Again. 'Two fry-ups and two flippin coffees!' It appeared we were fighting a losing battle.

An experience like that can cause you to lose confidence in your own memorability. Some time after, I went for a hair cut and said: 'I'll just have a bit off the top and the sides, bit longer at the back but please don't make it look like a mullet.' She said: '… the usual then?' I said: 'I didn't think I'd

The Joy of Ordering the Usual

been coming in here long enough.' She said: 'You've been coming here for years!' I said: 'Well, I used to go to this cafe and despite ordering the same thing every day, two fry-ups and two coffees, the bloke could never remember, but now that you've, you know, said it then... in future... I'll, erm.' The shop fell silent, embarrassment filled the air. I realised once again that in the wrong hands, mine, the art of ordering or being offered the usual can be a recipe for disaster.

But I've since realised that a simple trick can remove the risk and help you to look popular in your local chippy. When you order the usual, you should also tell them what it is. 'The usual please! Pudding chips and gravy.' Or in the newsagents: 'The usual please! This particular paper, a Twix and some of those sweets that stick in your teeth.' They then know what you want and you get to look like a regular, someone who's known and welcomed everywhere you go. After a while you'll even start to believe it yourself.

Of course there are some places where you don't want to be offered the usual. Chaps, in the lingerie shop when you're with your wife and she doesn't know you get dressed up and go out as Samantha every Thursday. Ladies, you wouldn't want a shop assistant to say, 'Ah, the usual!' as she drops anti-wrinkle cream into a bag. But do not fear the familiarity that comes with the usual. Embrace it. Especially if you've got no friends in your real life.

*

The Joy of Being Poetic

oetry, in motion, is pretty fantastic. I tend to read it on a bed at Tan-tastic. Shakespeare, Byron, I like all the greats. And once I've absorbed poems I show all my mates.

They call me a loser and tell me to stop embarrassing myself. That last bit isn't part of the poem, by the way. Unfortunately, philistines are what you encounter in droves if you're going to be poetic.

You see, if people struggle to string a sentence of short words together, it's unlikely they're capable of using long ones which rhyme. It's not your fault you're linguistically sophisticated and you should feel free to express yourself.

On occasion you'll write a line that sings. Sometimes you'll construct a verse that dances. And in magic moments you may conjure up a line so pretentious that it makes people want to slap you. The latter is what we're aiming for.

'The Cat Sat on the Mat' is quite possibly the greatest line of poetry ever written. It was a trailblazer and paved the way for other classics such as 'How Now Brown Cow?' and 'The Water in Majorca don't taste like what it Oughta'.

I'd suggest you let life's emotional journey inspire your

The Joy of Being Poetic

poetic expression with the pain of love and loss being particularly fruitful. One of my best poems is about losing my 'The A Team's BA Baracus' figure on holiday in Devon. It's called 'B A Comebacus' and, remarkably, manages to convey the devastation of our parting while still celebrating the joy of the twenty-two years we had together.

Talking of fruit, you won't read many poems about oranges. It's because the word doesn't actually rhyme with anything. Pear on the other hand rhymes with dare, share, wear and tear but, for some reason, there aren't many poems about pears either.

Why don't you make that your first poetic ditty? 'Pear Aware' is a possible title for you. You could saunter artistically over the majestic make-up of our country's fourth favourite fruit.

Despair. That's another word you can use which my wife has just suggested.

*

The Joy of Being Manly

The metrosexual male may be the new well-groomed kid on the block, but I reckon there's still room for a bit of manliness in modern society.

Some women would like to soften men's sharp edges. They want men to be more sensitive and understanding, more thoughtful and romantic and they'd happily have us sacrifice the ability to read maps to get there. 'Get in touch with your feminine side,' they say. 'Let's have a face mask and talk about our feelings.'

But it just so happens that lots of men, and I don't have to tell you that I'm among them, are proud to be strong and brave, honourable and hairy. We're men's men. We're the ones who take the bin out, at the third time of asking, and go downstairs at night if a light has been left on, if we really have to.

We're the ones who laugh hysterically at the salad menu in restaurants before ordering the steak or the mega meat combo challenge. And, by God, are we going to finish it.

The manly like their sport, cars and breasts, and drink pints not bottles. They sleep naked and consider the wearing

31

of jim-jams unthinkable. When they go to the gym they work the chest and arms, and then the arms and chest, and then finish with thirty sit-ups.

When entering any kind of public toilet, those who are manly do it with confidence and nod 'alright' without fear of misunderstanding. They choose the urinal in the middle, lean back as if that's necessary to keep their balance and make a 'woe-ahh!' noise, before finishing with an exaggerated shake.

You also have to be battle-hardened, so a scar or two is essential and it can't be from when your sister scratched you. I have a manly nose which isn't quite as perfect as nature intended but the cricket ball responsible won't be coming back for more, I'll tell you that for free.

However manly you are though, it may be that now and again you're obliged to re-establish your manliness in the eyes of the woman you love. I had to the other night when my wife went all doe-eyed at the sight of film star Matthew MacConaughy, lounging on a leather couch with his top off in an annoying TV advert for Dolche and Gabbana aftershave.

'Oooooh!' she said. 'Ooooh?' I countered. 'I'll knock him out next time I see him.'

And I will do. Next time I see him.

* The Joy of Being Literary

When I was about ten I had a shocking day at school. First I had diarrhoea, then I got tuberculosis and I finished off with psoriasis. That's a tough spelling test in anyone's book.

I took it in my stride though because I was a wordsmith and a bit of a geek. They used to call me the judge because I was always dishing out long sentences.

My vast knowledge of nine and twelve-letter words had come from reading books. To be literary you have to devour them and absorb them and that doesn't mean just looking at the pictures. Reading is food for the brain, in the same way that chocolate cake is food for the backside and I had a brain like the back end of a bus.

The best place to begin your literary journey is with the *Hungry Caterpillar* before moving onto the classics such as Dickens, the Brontë sisters and Jordon's fourth autobiography. By far her best, it's astonishing to think that, in coming centuries, literary scholars will discuss her use of prose and her acute ability to accentuate the allure of anecdotes through alliteration.

The Joy of Being Literary

Waxing lyrical about the book you're currently reading is essential, especially if it's something which is really hard work. *War and Peace* is the obvious I'm-only-reading-this-to-show-off book, but there are numerous others in the above two stones in weight category. Just don't expect anyone to care that you've finished one.

The real test of your literary prowess is whether you can write a book yourself and get more than just immediate family to buy it. It's said that everyone's got a book in them, although it's not necessarily one worth reading.

Some authors work with pen and paper but I prefer a computer because it's easier to delete whole sections. It does help if you know the grammatical nuances of the words you're using. An abstract noun, for example, is something you can see but can't touch, a bit like your older brother's skateboard when you're growing up.

Once your literary marvel is complete, all you need is a publisher who has the will to get to the end of your story and thinks it's worth repeating. If printing it yourself, it's probably best to test the market before you run off five thousand copies in hardback.

*

The Joy of Being Charming

When I was a young man and on the look out for love, me and a mate used to hit the town on a charm offensive. I'd be charming, he'd be offensive. He wondered why people took an instant dislike to him. I explained that it just saved time.

I, on the other hand, used to ooze charm from every orifice, so much so that I had big wet patches under my arms. I had to go out with Vaseline on my eyebrows to stop it dripping into my eyes and, on the dance floor, I used to spray charm on anyone nearby.

Once outside, I couldn't walk past a tree without all the birds in it swooping down to see me and many people I met just assumed I was a prince.

You see, charm is the ability to make somebody think you are both pretty wonderful. It's what everybody notices if you've got it and nobody notices if you haven't.

You have to be polite, respectful and complimentary and massage the ego of those in your charm zone (mine is about four metres square).

The Joy of Being Charming

Your ability to charm will depend in a large part on the amount of charisma you possess. It's a certain magnetism which can leave people spellbound but not everyone has it I'm afraid. A friend of mine is one of those unfortunate souls. He resigned himself to becoming an accountant when he realised he didn't have enough charisma to become an undertaker.

There are some people who are pretty resistant to charm and most of them work on reception desks. For some reason they just don't have the sensor which makes their knees go weak when you flash your teeth and say: 'Hey, beautiful.' Obviously, as a master of the art, these people eventually fall under my spell, but even I failed to charm on one occasion.

There was only one supermarket basket left at the door of the shop as a woman and I approached from separate directions. I said: 'You have that, sugar cheeks. I'm only after one thing.' 'Typical male,' she mumbled to herself, as she walked away.

Charming, I thought.

*

The Joy of Being Dismissive

W hen in the hands of a dismissive master, this art can be one of the most delicate and subtle skills in the shops today. I'm guessing it's probably beyond you, but I may as well tell you anyway.

As with most skills, there are varying levels and a novice may dive in at the deep end and start being 'very dismissive', only one rung down from 'completely'. Then there's 'pretty' and 'kind of' dismissive, but the one I'd suggest you employ is 'a little'. Jumping in there with two big feet and openly saying what you actually think is the last thing you're intending to do.

Being dismissive is not very honourable. It's basically a coward's way of criticising. You're fleetingly disparaging, hinting that you're unimpressed and then when your subject looks at you desperately for reassurance, you give it to them, even though you're lying through your teeth.

The whole point of being a little dismissive is that you never actually show your cards, you just momentarily imply that you think the other person's hand is rubbish. Being

The Joy of Being Dismissive

dismissive never stands up to interrogation because its strength is in its aloofness. If you're forced into confirming that you have no faith in your chubby brother to run a marathon, you've actually gone beyond dismissive and stumbled into honesty.

The target of a real connoisseur will never be certain about what has just happened. It's a fluttering of negativity, the beat of a butterfly's wing, which the recipient won't really be sure if they heard or not.

What really sets your dismissive comment or look in stone is the denial that must follow. 'What? Of course I think you can do it! Why wouldn't I believe you could win *Britain's Got Talent*?' If they are looking at you with heartbroken eyes, I'd suggest you fly into a wild cackle, shake your head hysterically and slap them on the back while saying: 'Come on! As if I'd doubt you!'

Tragically, people who are dismissive are often living in fear themselves. It's easier to dismiss someone else's hopes and dreams than to acknowledge that they themselves live a life of unfulfilled misery. If only someone had believed in them when they were younger, perhaps now they could believe in others.

But if you feel being dismissive is a bridge to far for you, and I'm not for a second saying it is, perhaps you'd be better suited to some other activity. Have you ever tried drinking excessively? Most people can manage that.

*

The Joy of Gossip

G ossiping is basically the sharing or spreading of what could be considered sought after information. It's usually intimate or sensational and is great fun, as long as you're not the subject of it.

Essentially your revelations should be new, but all good gossip also has a shock value. You need to locate your local grapevine because this is where it grows. To harvest really juicy morsels you also need to nurture the grapevine with titbits of your own. Give gossip freely and it will flow back in return.

Your ears always need to be pricked up for the next big revelation. When rumours spread like wildfire, it's your job to be there wafting the flames at the beginning and the more scandalous they are, the better. Remember, being first with the news is always more important than being factually correct.

'You're not going to believe this…' is the best way to introduce gossip. And when preparing to dispense it, it's customary to perform an obvious and exaggerated look

The Joy of Gossip

around to check for spies before leaning forward into your gossip delivery pose.

What you want is a reaction like: 'Never!' or 'Give over, that's astonishing!' What you don't want is: 'Oh yes, I know. Jenny told me that last week.' If this happens regularly, a wholesale review of your access to the grapevine may be required.

Malicious gossip is a rumour which just might be true spread enthusiastically by those who would do the subject harm. It can damage relationships and reputations and shouldn't be passed on unless it's an absolute cracker.

Of course, gossiping is nothing new and it's not very nice. In ancient Greece, the great philosopher Socrates was widely lauded for his wisdom and his disdain for gossips.

If someone approached him with idle tittle-tattle he would demand they pass the Test of Three. The first test being whether they knew for sure it was true, the second being whether it was something good and the third test was whether it was useful. Unless the answer was yes to all three, he didn't want to hear it.

This is the reason Socrates was a great philosopher and held in such high esteem. It also explains why he never found out that Plato was sleeping with his wife. But you didn't hear that from me.

*

The Joy of Romance

The concept of romance was developed by women in the middle ages as a stick to beat men with. Romance, or more particularly a lack or it, has been responsible for arguments and break-ups ever since.

Women believe it's their right and find it astonishing that men just don't get it. In response, men fear romance and have convinced themselves that it's foreign to them, a language that only those flippin' smooth Italian men know about, or care to know about.

But the truth is being romantic is easy for men, if they're prepared to put a bit of thought into it. It's a science rather than an art and it can be reduced to a simple equation. 'Present + surprise = extended spell in the good books'. Unfortunately, for all concerned, the way it usually happens is: 'Extended spell in bad books + present = well, I hope you don't think that makes up for it'.

The key element here is surprise, as long as the surprise isn't that it's the day after your anniversary. It could be a diamond necklace or a packet of Minstrels you bought at a

The Joy of Romance

petrol station, the romantic value is exactly the same. Any lady would be equally happy with either of those.

Admittedly, being romantic can be time-consuming. Fifty balloons bearing the words 'I love you!' don't blow themselves up. Planting enough tulips to spell the words 'Pudding Bum' on a motorway banking is recommended, but could be disappointingly inaccurate following a bad frost. Have faith though. Persistence should one day pay off and your reward will be your partner's happiness. On average this lasts for about two days per romantic gesture.

So fellas, here are three sure fire winners... 1: Get yourself a packet of Rolos and save her the last one. Always works. 2: If you're out for a meal and the greasy guy with roses comes round, buy her one! It's only a pound. 3: Keep your eye out for videos like 'Chris De Burgh live in concert' in the bargain bins, especially if she wears red a lot.

A word of warning though. If after years of pleading complete ignorance to romance, you begin surprising her with cards saying she's your 'one and only' and flowers you picked in a field, she'll probably decide you've been up to no good. Plus this is a marathon not a sprint, so don't begin at a pace you can't sustain. You definitely want to avoid setting the standard so high that the woman in your life is expecting a romantic gesture every month.

✳

The Joy of Matchmaking

A h, singletons. Poor, poor singletons. Sat, flicking through the TV guide, wondering what to wear for their date with a microwave meal.

If you're a bit smug because you're in a relationship, even if it's a bad one, a good way to get a bit of spark back into your life is by inflicting your superiority on a single friend by volunteering to find them a soulmate.

A complete lack of enthusiasm from your new project should in no way put you off. I'd also completely ignore any suggestions that they're happy as they are or that they're enjoying their freedom. They're single so what do they know anyway?

Of course, you don't want to set them up with just any old duffer so it's best to do a bit of research before you start looking for suitable companions.

The first question is, 'How desperate are you?'

Whatever the answer to this, always assume they are playing down the true state of their loneliness and despair. In fact, as you get your clipboard out they're probably

The Joy of Match-making

looking at you and wondering what's wrong with them. We'll soon find out.

Once you've given them a desperation rating between one and five, you can start to get a picture of their likes and dislikes. Is it men, women or goats? Do they enjoy staying in or staying out, walking in the rain or drinking tequila?

By now it will be glaringly obvious why they're single and it is most likely to be because they're expecting too much. Give it to them straight. It's either looks or personality. It's greedy to want both, although you'll have to admit, humbly, that you've managed to pull it off.

Arrange a date and if romance blossoms you can claim all the credit. If it doesn't, well, the hunt continues. Don't give up, especially if the single person insists; it's not really up to them after all.

The dream for all matchmakers is that one of their introductions ends up in marriage. There are few things more wonderful than to sit down at a wedding knowing you're going to get a little thank you in the speech for bringing the happy couple together. Job done, on to your next victim.

And where better to find them than at a wedding? As the night goes on, you'll begin to spot those who would benefit from your expertise. They'll either be sharking round the dance floor or under a table. Those under the table will be in no position to refuse your offer, so I'd target them first.

*

The Joy of Saying Sorry

S ay what you want about the amount of money Elton John spends on flowers, but you can't deny he can hit the nail on the head when it comes to writing songs.

With 'Candle in the Wind' he summed up the tragedy of Marilyn Monroe's lonely demise with sensitivity and understanding. When he rewrote it in 1997, following the death of another iconic woman, he was again spot on. I'm sure Mother Teresa would have loved 'Sandals in the Bin', had she been around to hear it.

But when it comes to sorry being the hardest word, I have to disagree with Elton. It can be annoying when you really don't want to say it because, actually, you're not sorry at all, but generally it rolls of the tongue.

'Sorry I'm late'. 'Sorry to bother you'. 'Sorry about that, I thought they knew. I'm sure you'll find another job.'

The word is instilled in us from an early age as the antidote to anything that goes wrong, mainly because it's much easier than teaching toddlers to say: 'I'd like apologise for one's behaviour.' As a result, it's so overused in polite

45

The Joy of Saying Sorry

society that it may take a few added extras to convince anyone you genuinely mean it.

For a start, you need to avoid smiling, smirking or shrugging your shoulders in the preceding moments. Then I'd recommend a slightly furrowed brow and, depending on the severity of your *faux pas*, a little disappointed sigh and shake of the head to suggest a mild bout of self-loathing.

But the secret weapon of saying sorry is inserting the words, 'really, really' in front of it. It'll be a stubborn mule indeed who dismisses your apology with that build up. Sometimes my little girl manages to pull it off with such sincerity that I just want to hold her and say: 'It's ok my princess. You can put my keys in the bin whenever you feel like it.'

There may be rare occasions when even three or four reallys won't do the job. If a bit of sobbing doesn't work either, it could be that the damage you've done is beyond repair.

Holding a grudge won't do your victim any good in the long run though. If you've been wronged and you're refusing to accept someone's apology, you're only extending your own pain as the bitterness is left to fester inside your heart. I usually find that forgiveness, and a healthy out-of-court settlement, will set you both free.

Which reminds me of what Elton says in another of his classics. 'It's no sacrifice, just a simple word. It's two hearts living, in two separate worlds'. If I'm honest, I'm not entirely sure what he's banging on about with that one.

The Joy of Letter Writing

The art of letter writing is in extreme danger. Emails and social networking have rendered the practice of taking a pen and scribing words on a piece of paper almost archaic.

If you type a letter on a computer it might be nicely laid out but where's the personal touch? Where's that mark from when you choked on a bit of chocolate bourbon as you were writing and spat it on the page? Where's that bit where you crossed out three attempts at spelling 'hemeroyds' and then wrote 'piles' instead?

Twenty years ago everyone had a letter writing set for thank you notes and correspondence with long-distance relatives and the building society. Children had pen friends because schools were twinned with those in another part of the world and letters were exchanged to help them appreciate that not everyone is as lucky as them. My pen friend lived in Rochdale.

These days the only traditional pen friend relationships that continue to exist are those between serial killers and random women who couldn't find a man in their local pub. I'm guessing the main reason the cons write back is because they can't claim they didn't have the time while in prison.

Writing letters of complaint can be rewarding. You should always attempt to sound hurt yet superior, pointing out in minute detail the impact of you being wronged in such an insensitive and heartless way. I then move on to what I'd like in compensation, be it an apology, money or a just to be allowed back into the house.

Love letters should include a few more niceties. This is a perfect place to unleash compliments so over the top you'd be embarrassed to say them in person. I'd always advise you get the name right, put a bit of poetry in there if you can and don't be afraid to lay your feelings bare. For example: 'I love your smile and I love your bum, but I sometimes worry you'll look like your mum'.

On occasion a letter is the bearer of bad news. My mate recently arrived home to find a note from his wife on the kitchen table. It read: 'You never notice me or talk to me anymore and you certainly don't act like you love me. Yesterday I had my best knickers on and you just watched TV then fell asleep. Either you're cheating on me or you don't want me, so I'm off.

'P.S. Don't try to find me. I'm moving away to Duckinfield with your brother.'

As you can imagine, much of my time is spent reading the one piece of fan mail which has flooded in since I began writing my newspaper column. I say fan mail. It was more a note to point out a grammatical error, but pleasant all the same. To be fair though, I struggle to read it. That's the trouble with handwritten letters isn't it?

*

The Joy of Being Vain

ey there, good looking. I'm guessing you didn't check over your shoulder to see if I meant someone else. Why would you, what with those cheekbones and eyes? You didn't get those at Pound Land, oh no.

Your beauty is a gift from God and he was feeling particularly kind that day. To be fair though, he's balanced it out with your lack of personality but you can't have everything.

Lets not kid ourselves here, you are a bit of a looker and the world is a prettier place because of it.

Vanity, if you're handsome, is something to be embraced. It's your right as one of the chosen few to be admired, envied and desired and, as you well know, it breeds understandable confidence.

On a recent night out, I gave the girl in a nightclub cloakroom a seductive wink and said: 'Tell you what, there are some smoothies in here tonight.' She said: 'There's one less than you seem to think.' I winked again, ran my fingers across my stick-on hairy chest (I had got that from Pound

The Joy of Being Vain

Land), and glided into the night, feeling generous for the charm and beauty I'd just bestowed on her.

Most seriously vain people fall in love with themselves at an early age and stay faithful for life. I bet they think that song is about them, they're so vain. I bet they think that song is about them, don't they, don't they?

It takes the vain hours to do their hair and make-up. It takes them days to walk past a mirror. After all, mirrors are Gods way of speaking directly to them. When they're gazing at their reflection, it's said the moment of clarity when they catch that sparkle in their eye is something ugly people can only dream of.

If you're going to be really vain, it's fine and even encouraged to admit it openly and brashly. But you aren't allowed to laugh at yourself at all. You'd never be seen with a hair out of place, let alone wearing silly glasses and a false nose, even if you were undercover.

Unsurprisingly, vanity can be a smokescreen for a lack of confidence. Vain people are often telling themselves they're beautiful because they're worried no one else will. Or they are frightened that if people look beyond the pretty exterior they'll find a big void of emptiness where the real person is supposed to be.

In the end, of course, it's what's on the inside that counts. I have to admit though, I have a feeling my insides are pretty good looking as well.

*

The Joy of Being Emotional

T he world of emotion is changing. Historically, it was women who excelled at this skill and the only time a man could cry was when his football team got relegated or when England lost on penalties.

Any bloke showing even a hint emotion for any other reason would have been given a good slap to bring him round. Now though, the barriers have come down and male tears are flowing freely.

Psychologists believe men's readiness to acknowledge their feelings is good for society and the main cause is the encouragement they've had from reality TV. By the second series of *X Factor* every contestant was having an emotional breakdown, whether they got through or Simon told them they were an embarrassment to their family. Programmes like *Wife Swap* also taught us that it's ok to admit you love the person you live with, even if they treat you like a slave.

If you're a modern man you've got to let it all out. Perhaps your wife or girlfriend has said something insensitive. I agree that it's not your fault if you can't read a

The Joy of Being Emotional

map unless you're pointing it in the direction you're travelling in. But it has ruffled feathers. Many women now feel compelled to be even more emotional, fearful that men are stepping on their toes. I'm told some worry that men will be after 'unreasonable' and 'irrational' next.

If you're going to get emotional then it means feelings of sadness or joy overwhelm you and, because it's not the done thing in Britain, when it really kicks in you have to shake your head and waft air at your eyes as if that might blow the emotion back in.

Tears of joy are much more fun than tears of sadness and weddings are a great place to release the former. The father of the bride cries, all the women do too, even if they've just come in off the street and don't know the couple. Often, the groom will be sobbing uncontrollably as he contemplates the rest of his life in the headlock of love. It's just such a happy occasion.

Awards ceremonies are now blubber central as well and it's usually the audience who are upset, as they're forced to listen the winner drone on about the amazing assistant who deserves to share in their glory. I'd recommend a little emotion induced sniffle but 'doing a Gwyneth' is to be avoided, especially if all you've won is the Employee of the Month award at Pound Land.

Having said all this about the brave new world, there is one arena where men still refuse to let their emotions get to them… reunions. If a woman sees her long lost friend across a crowded room, she'll run over and hug them and say how great it is to see them.

If you're a man and you see your best friend for the first time in twenty years, you shout, 'Oi tosser!' and give him the V's.

Some things are still sacred after all.

*

The Joy of Being Organised

I n this country, being organised is seen as a route to success. In other places, such as France, it's seen as boring and lacking in Gaelic flair. Across the channel, being unpredictable is as important as not washing, but the British think if you're organised there's a good chance you'll be on time and that usually goes down well.

If you've been stumbling through life acting as if things can be put off until tomorrow, the fun is over. First we're going to organise your thoughts, then we're going to organise your arms and legs because, only then, can you put your CDs in alphabetical order.

If you're organised it means that you decide what needs doing and get it done. It also means you book holidays three years in advance and generally carry a clipboard just in case you need one.

To organise yourself you'll first have to make some tough decisions, which are the ones you've probably been trying to avoid. Then you're ready to start taking actions which need to be prioritised in order of importance and I'd suggest you get a special pen for writing lists. To-do lists,

The Joy of Being Organised

have-been-meaning-to-do lists, should-really-have-done lists and of course, list lists, which contain the details of all your other lists.

Sitting down probably shouldn't appear on a list. Nor should having a nice glass of wine. Mind you, when I was unemployed I put everything I did on a list just so I could tick it off and keep my spirits up. 1. Have a cup of tea. 2. Lie on settee for bit. 3. Watch *Loose Women*. 4. Get job. I reasoned that three out of four wasn't bad for a Wednesday.

As you tick things off your lists, you'll feel better about yourself and before you know it there'll be a structure to your life, which means its run like a military operation. It might not sound like a barrel of laughs, but when you open your fridge to find everything in colour-coded tubs you'll know it's all been worth it.

Women, by their very nature, are better organised and like to believe that men couldn't sort out a piss up in a brewery. I think most men would be happy to give it a go.

The organising peak of a woman's life will be her wedding. A few days before mine, my fiancée was getting a bit worked up about it all and said she was worried she'd forgotten some insignificant detail. Her mum said: 'Don't worry, the best man will make sure he turns up.'

Embrace the new 'organised you' but be prepared to reminisce about those final demands you no longer receive. And don't get too carried away and devise a system so sophisticated it's impossible to find anything again once it's been filed. My wife even filed me once and I was only discovered again when the time came to tax her car.

*

The Joy of Being Passionate

I n ancient Greece, they didn't bother with epitaphs or obituaries. When a man died they just asked one question... Did he have passion? Which is why, in those days, it was a pretty handy skill to have if you wanted to be remembered for more than five minutes.

If you intend to convince people you're passionate then you can't do it half-heartedly. You have to at least appear like you're putting your heart and soul into it because that's what others expect. People with a passion are often envied by those who lack one but, be warned, sometimes it takes so much effort you'll wish you hadn't bothered.

Pick your passion carefully and crucially, make sure it doesn't take too much dedication. I'd suggest you avoid passions like mountain climbing or achieving world peace. Passionately eating fish fingers every Tuesday is much more achievable.

It's always important for people to see your disappointment when you're prevented from following your passion but, once it's well established, I'd always refuse to talk about it. It adds a bit of mystery and superiority and

The Joy of Being Passionate

besides, you don't want to bore people any more than you already do.

Being 'passionately in love' is all very well as long as both parties are in agreement that's what's actually going on. Passion can quickly become obsession, especially if the victim of your desire refuses to ring you back. And you'd be surprised how quickly they can get a restraining order these days.

There are a few pretenders for passion's crown which you should be wary of. The poor man's passion is enthusiasm. The idea that turning up and trying hard at something constitutes a skill in the same way passion does is a bit upsetting for someone as passionate about being passionate as I am. The phrase 'you're keen aren't you?' should set alarm bells ringing straight away. If you carry on you're in real danger of being thought of as over-enthusiastic. That's one step worse and code for embarrassing.

My own particular passion is Spaghetti alla Carbonara. I've walked out of Italian restaurants when it wasn't on the menu. I had it twice in one day in Rome and then for breakfast on another day in Prague. That was the best one ever. The thought of it makes my mouth water and my heart sing and, in quiet moments, I imagine myself in a room full of countless bowls of Carbonara, each one made by a different chef, an eternity of creamy bacon pasta delights.

Thankfully, it's a passion I'm in control of, which brings me to another valid point. Don't become so passionate you end up looking stupid. Unless of course, looking stupid is your chosen passion. You wouldn't be alone in that.

*

The Joy of Being Over-dramatic

The first time I was accused of being over dramatic, I nearly hit the deck. After all those years of staying calm, once or twice, it felt like a knife through my heart. My whole life began to flash before me and if I do say so myself, it was breathtaking.

All those moments when I'd thrown myself just a bit too far back when our cat swung for me. The time when I said we should move house because I had 'a feeling' only to change my mind when I had 'a feeling' that we shouldn't move five minutes later. And that day when I realised someone had put sugar in my tea and I spat it all over the fireplace. I only have sugar in coffee, you see.

Could it be that they were right? Of course it could. Like most over-dramatics I'd started young and worked hard to keep it up.

That time when my brother hit a seven-year-old me with a bag of marbles, it didn't actually hurt. But he still doesn't get pudding whenever I bring it up at family meals. When my wife requested I take the bin out last night, I hadn't actually been shot either.

The Joy of Being Over-dramatic

The key to being over-dramatic isn't so much what happens to you, it's how you over react to what happens to you. With a desperate look or a stunned gasp for air, you need to convey that what's just been said or done changes everything. Or at least it does for a few seconds until you realise you're just being silly.

Always deny being over-dramatic as if you life depends on it. I'm guessing you're flabbergasted anyone could suggest such a thing, so tell them so and if there's a room to storm out of then you go ahead and do it.

After a while, over-egging the pudding should become second nature. At the slightest tickle of a fish bone you'll grab your throat and look around desperately, only to miraculously survive and help yourself to the last piece of broccoli. You'll be completely blown away by every piece of slightly interesting news you hear. The less interesting it is, the more hurricane-like that gust of wind will have to be.

Once up to speed, if you're not having a couple of near-death experiences a week, then you're not doing it properly. I can have three or four on a good week. Honestly, I'm not being over-dramatic.

✳

The Joy of Being an Animal Lover

Y ou've got to love animals. It's their puppy dog eyes (dogs), their kitten cat nose (cats) and their cheeky little chops (pigs).

Some people love them more than they love humans and with good reason. They don't answer back, they won't judge you and they'll love you unconditionally on the condition that you feed them.

For many, animals aren't just pets, they're part of the family and they're much more popular than some members. They do whatever they want but you wee in the corner of the front room and all of a sudden it's a major crime.

We're said to be a nation of dog lovers and the best one I've seen is half-rottweiler and half-sheepdog. It will rip your arm off then go and get help.

If you ever need one, dogs are a great excuse to go for a walk in the rain while swinging a bag of warm muck at six o'clock in the morning.

They're known as man's best friend because of their loyalty, whereas cats are more like that friend who only rings you when they want something. Even then they tut and say

59

The Joy of Being an Animal Lover

things like, 'Why would you do that?' when you tell them what you've been up to.

You should generally start your animal loving with a goldfish before moving onto rabbits, tortoises, horses and giraffes. Fish are ok but not great for conversation. Tortoises are fun until you realise they're going to outlive you. Horses save on petrol but make some men feel inadequate. Get a giraffe though and it's win win. You've got a friend with worse pyjamas than you and they can earn their keep cleaning out gutters.

Your love can be called into question if you ever have to take an animal to the vets. It may tug on your heart strings to see your tortoise using little crutches, but when you get the bill you'll probably decide he can just stay still for the next eighty years.

Even so, it can be very upsetting to lose a treasured pet. My brother had terrible luck with hamsters. His first one died tragically when it fell asleep at the wheel, then Hammo's replacement became seriously ill. My mum was so worried about how my brother would cope with its impeding death that she promised him a big party to celebrate its life. He said: 'Brilliant. Can we kill it now?'

Most animals have been around longer than us and great and small, every one of them is special. My personal favourite is a cow which lives in a field near me. It appears beautiful and intelligent and whenever I wave it gazes back at me with a twinkle in its eye. If only it could talk, I'm sure it would say something like, 'What?'

*

The Joy of Being Honest

ome people would say that honesty is the foundation on which a respectable society is built. The idiots! They've obviously never left a shop before realising they've been given too much change. Woo hoo! You're £1.73 up and you've stuck two fingers up to the corporate giants who rule our lives! Unless it's just a small family business. Then you may start to feel a bit bad as you dive into your car and start the engine quicker than ever before.

The reason for this guilt is your conscience. It's what hurts when all your other parts feel really good and it's why a good majority of people stick to being honest, more often than not.

Being honest demands that you be fair and just and deal in fact, not fiction. You shouldn't cheat or steal and your word should be your bond. If possible you should be as honest as the day is long. That's a summer day, not one in December. You have to live and die by the sword of truthfulness, just ask any politician.

It's not like you have much choice anyway because the

The Joy of Being Honest

need for honesty was probably ingrained in you from a young age. It's drilled into children from the moment they start lying which is why telling lies is so much more exciting.

It's doesn't have to be all holier than thou righteousness though, because one of the best uses for honesty is to insult people. It has such a protective force that if you hide behind it you can say almost anything. 'Can I be honest with you? I really used to hate you but now I just think you're a bit of a saddo.' Mesmerised by your honesty, it's likely they'll say they appreciate it.

'Brutal honesty' is the next rung up and should be used sparingly for things like shattering a person's dreams. 'To be brutally honest, you're rubbish and you always have been.' In years to come when they're still scrabbling round, trying to pick up the pieces of their life, they'll probably reflect that your honesty had a refreshing quality about it.

When it comes to relationships, being honest is at the top of a woman's wishlist after jewellery, chocolates and surprise weekends away. Even when under pressure though, a man should never tell a woman that he's unworthy of her love. She already knows.

There are times when honesty is not to be advised and poor judgement can have terrible consequences. Spare a thought for the man who ended up in casualty with a bloody nose and two black eyes. When the doctor asked him what had happened he reasoned that whoever said, 'honesty is the best policy' was not married to a woman with an enormous behind.

*

The Joy of Being Flexible

S ome people can't see the point of being flexible. They say if God had wanted them to touch their toes, he'd have put them on their knees. Plus, they think there's no need to spend hours stretching individual muscles if they can get up in a morning, put their arms in the air and do their entire body at once while making an 'Arrryuuuurrrrggghh!' noise.

But they underestimate the power of flexibility. It's not just about bending down to reach your toes, it includes things like getting back up again as well, and the further you stretch, the more flexible you'll become. Within a year or two you'll be able to put your legs behind your head, which is as useful today as it always has been.

Your basic options for increasing flexibility are yoga and pilates. Yoga is excellent for un-kinking the muscles, which means it's great if you're really kinky. Pilates is for people who think they're a bit too flash for yoga.

Getting into the correct position is essential. That's why the serenity of a class is often interrupted by the teacher

The Joy of Being Flexible

shouting things like 'Knees up, Carol!' or 'Who was that?' Most sessions end with a short spell of meditation to centre one's inner self and put off getting up. It's got to be better than sitting around doing nothing.

Away from your non-slip mat, having a flexible attitude will help you navigate your way through life without being destroyed by what some may consider slight disappointment. Having a rigid viewpoint is similar to having a stiff neck. So, roll with the punches, don't get hung up if things don't always go to plan and, if things get really bad, why not try dropping into the flying crow pose wherever you are?

Finally, a flexible partner in the bedroom is what most men's dreams are made of. They imagine they'll have the night of their life with a woman capable of enchanting them with the riches of the *Kama Sutra*. Once in bed though, and especially if it's a week night, it's more than likely the man's flexibility which will be called into action. Otherwise, the last-minute cancellation of proceedings due to an unexpected headache could ruin his night.

If this happens a lot in your house, you might be better off signing up for a pilates class instead.

*

The Joy of Being Sophisticated

ophistication isn't something for which the British are well known anymore. It might be to do with our reputation for football hooliganism and being sick on nights out.

You've got to be cool, cultured and clever, distinguished and debonair.

You have to casually dip Ferrero Rochers in your brew as you flick through a copy of *Woman's Own* or *Men and Motors* on your antique carved ming coffee table.

You may also find youself eating a Bounty in an overflowing bath while making witty and cutting comments to an imaginary butler in between mouthfuls. When your partner bursts in and screams that you've flooded the front room below, I'd recommend you treat them to a nonchalant and knowing shrug as you announce, 'Je ne sais pas. Pourquoi?'

Crucially, to be sophisticated you have to believe that you are. It comes with an air of arrogance.

You don't doubt yourself. Why would you?

The Joy of Being Sophisticated

You're educated and worldly-wise. You can order an ice cream on your holidays in Spain without shouting.

Developing sophisticated tastes is something you'll have to work at because caviar is disgusting the first twenty times you try it. Before long though you'll be drinking red wine costing more than four pounds a bottle and not just so you can get hammered.

But I'd suggest the best thing to start your training with is canapés.

For me they are the definition of sophistication. Decadent and cosmopolitan, yet mysterious and ridiculous, the whole point is that you can't tell what they are from looking at them.

With the first one you'll have a little nibble, but once you realise they just crumble everywhere when you do that you'll start shoving them in whole. Etiquette demands you only take one at a time but there's nothing to stop you following the waiter.

My wife and I tend to have them every Sunday evening. When it's just us, we have to take turns walking round the front room with the tray.

*

The Joy of Being Modest

I f there's one thing I'm good at, it's acting modestly. For me, modesty isn't so much an art form as a way of life.

Believe me, I spend a lot of my time trying to deflect compliments with a shrug of the shoulders or an embarrassed smile. It can be quite exhausting, always being ready to play down my achievements or chuckle meekly and claim it wasn't really down to me.

I wouldn't say being modest is fun. It's a selfless act, call it a charitable gift to your friends and colleagues. Sometimes I just want to crack and say: 'Yes, you're right. I am brilliant.' But the last person anyone wants to spend time with is an arrogant big head, so you need to constantly throw them off the scent.

I'd suggest that half the skill of being modest is to always expect praise. Often you'll see a compliment coming and when it inevitably arrives, you're prepared for it and can immediately suggest that really someone else should take the plaudits.

The Joy of Being Modest

But the real key is in the sincerity you can muster. Your denial must cling to the possibility that you honestly aren't aware of your qualities. The worst thing in the world is to be accused of false modesty, so an expression of surprise is recommended. But don't overdo it with the shocked head shaking. You could end up giving the game away.

On occasion your modesty mettle will be tested by someone who's pretty insistent. 'Come on,' they'll say for the third time. 'Admit it, you're a legend.' If an exclamation of bewilderment still doesn't do the trick, I tend to fall back on a slightly pressured laugh. 'Honestly…' I say, like I'm really beginning to tire of this charade. I then indicate with my eyes that they won't break me, it's time to stop.

If being modest is an activity you're planning to take up I'd suggest that to get up to speed you go looking for compliments. Set up situations where you can save the day, only to deny any involvement moments later.

I can guess what you're thinking now. Probably, 'Wow! You're something else, Kev.'

Stop it! You're embarrassing me! Seriously. Stop it.

*

The Joy of Being Tough

ometimes it's hard being tough. Rock hard. But I say if the cap fits, wear it while doing one-arm press-ups.

There is physical toughness (on occasion I hit a punch bag in the gym without gloves) and mental toughness (the other night I resisted opening another packet of Jammy Dodgers) and really you need to excel in both.

You have to be made of sterner stuff, chiselled out of granite and a bit like an old pair of boots. You don't have to wear a badge letting everyone know, it should be obvious. But if, like me, you'd bought one before you knew that was one of the rules, you may as well wear it anyway. Mine says 'Buns of Steel!', which does have a nice ring to it.

Badge or not, I'd recommend a constant aura of invincibility which suggests that if a wild bear suddenly appeared you could effortlessly wrestle it to the ground and Sellotape its mouth shut. I've only actually had to do that once but you've always got to be ready, just in case.

There are plenty of arenas in which to showcase your toughness. From arm wrestling you can progress to naked

The Joy of Being Tough

mud wrestling and from there you can start walking on hot coals on a weekend or play Extreme Trivial Pursuits.

While violence is something I'd never condone, on occasion the tough do have to stand up and be counted. My performance in the one and only rumble I've had on the rugby pitch is still discussed at length by my team mates.

'Every time I pulled one off you, Kev, another jumped on!' one lad still remembers fondly. My fighting style, 'The Windmill' as it's now known, hasn't been employed since by anyone and that's probably for the best. Lets just say there must have been some pretty sore knuckles that day and they certainly weren't mine.

Other signs of toughness are taking bottle tops off with your teeth, having tattoos on your forehead and drinking black coffee. I've got one pal who likes to say: 'Coffee please, black. And make it as strong as you like.' Which means I then have to use a particularly deep voice when ordering my decaf-latte.

But however tough you are, there's always someone tougher. Usually, it's your mother. Many a hardcase has fallen silent when he's been clipped round the ear. Especially when it's followed by: 'And there's another one where that came from.'

*

The Joy of Positive Thinking

A nyone who has the ability to think has the potential to think positively. Trouble is, the negative thoughts can be so much more convincing. What you have to do is ride against the tide and all the evidence and banish the idea that you're a waste of space.

It's not that you're hopeless, you've just had a bad run of luck. 'But there's no such thing as luck!' it says here in this life-changing manual. Well, actually, there is, but it turns out you have to make it yourself.

The entire positive thinking phenomenon is built on slogans so really you need to learn a few and start chanting them before breakfast. Here are some suggestions... 'Success breeds success' (Charles Darwin). 'The Winner takes it all' (Abba). 'You've got to be in it to Win it' (National Lottery adverts).

Very important is not giving up, especially when it appears all hope is gone. In fact, that's really the time when you should come into your own as the self-delusion reaches fever pitch.

The Joy of Positive Thinking

Remember: 'If at first you don't succeed, try, try again.' Tell that to the person who's just taken up skydiving. 'But winners never quit and quitters never win!' so peel yourself up off the tarmac and sort out your attitude (and your altitude).

On the road to success there's no room for excuses. 'I don't care if you've fallen ten thousand feet to your death. What that actually meant was you had an opportunity for greatness, a bit of time to visualise the perfect landing and a sizable chunk of motivation. Unfortunately you spent most of the way down crying.'

Alternatively, there is the softer style of encouragement. I could suggest that, on reflection, you ought not to have picked up the wrong rucksack by accident and, with a bit more concentration and urgent reincarnation, you could do better next time. Equally pointless but a little more British.

Affirmation is vital to convincing yourself you're a world beater and if you're not sure what it means then just keep telling yourself you are.

There can, of course, come a time when you're sick of being positive all the time. You just crave a bit of honesty and deep down hope someone will put you out of your misery and tell you to not to bother.

If that's how you feel you could just make friends with people who are much less successful than you. All of a sudden you'll find you're not doing that badly and you'll realise the route to happiness is in knowing life's not about having what you want, it's about wanting what you have. There's no better slogan than that.

*

The Joy of Being Understood

'Mercy bucket.' I said, pretty chuffed that I was fluent after just three days in Francais. 'Oui mon petite pois,' I continued, delivering the language with the confidence and panache of a 72-year-old woman who'd spent her entire life in a village near Lyon playing boules.

There had been one or two misunderstandings along the way. Like the time I went into the perfume shop looking for the aftershave 'Joop'. 'C'est rouge,' I explained (it's red) to a blanc (white) looking face (mush). 'Pour home?' I said. 'Non!' she replied, looking slightly panicky that she was alone in the shop with me. It was only afterwards I found out I'd been asking for a red skirt for a man.

Then there was the time I asked a horrified barman in the Pyrenees if he had Aids. I tried again and added: 'Avec pommes?' Turns out the word for cider is dangerously close to that of the killer disease.

And it's not just across the Channel where they don't immediately understand me. When I was in need of directions in Wales once I pulled over to speak to a farmer

The Joy of Being Understood

who was standing by the side of the road. 'Are you shearing that sheep?' I asked, trying to make conversation. He said: 'No. Get your own.'

I started to think that I was the problem and my wife was happy to confirm that was true. She said she'd struggled to understand me for years. My quirky little freakish traits, like how I can't touch bread muffins with flour on and how I still haven't realised that when she leaves something on the stairs she wants me to take it upstairs rather than climb over it. More than anything she claims to be left baffled by me thinking my opinion would be appreciated.

The best way to ensure you're understood is to keep it simple. Be honest and consistent and true to yourself. When communicating use small words and try to speak with a mouth that isn't full of food. Shout as if everyone is deaf and point at things so it's clear to what you are referring. Sometimes, despite your best efforts, it will feel like you're talking a different language, but if you will go to Greece on holiday then you should really expect that.

Occasionally, however, it's nice to be misunderstood. With children, it can lead to the loveliest of conversations. My daughter once started asking me about teeth as I read her a bedtime story.

'Do doggies have teeth?' she asked. 'Yes they do,' I said. 'What else?' 'Cats have teeth…' 'And crocodiles?' 'Yes they do,' I said. Then, all in one go, she wondered: 'What about the ceiling and the triangle and the doors and the sky and a flower?' 'No they don't,' I replied. 'It's just animals.'

She thought about it… 'What about my trampoline?'

*The Joy of Being Eco-Friendly

I f there is one favour it would be nice to do for your great-great-grandchildren, it would be to save the world so that they don't have to move into outer space.

We can only do this if we're not washed away by a flood or burnt to a crisp by an unexpected heat wave, so it would appear we have to get friendly with the environment and the eco-system that keeps it stable.

It may be that climate change has already gone beyond the point of no return for much of the UK but, in true British style, you can switch to low energy light bulbs and have a jolly good go at stopping it anyway.

What do you mean it's pointless because China keeps opening hundreds of huge new factories? Well, every little bit counts. You can only worry about your own carbon footprint and, besides, how else could we buy trainers so cheaply?

If you're going to take up eco-friendliness then the key is to reduce the amount of energy you use. This means spending most of the day on the settee and moving only

The Joy of Being Eco-Friendly

when absolutely necessary. If the heating's on too high or you can't reach the TV remote, that's just tough. Personal sacrifice is what's needed to protect the planet.

My grandad was an environmentalist so it's in my blood. He was always saying 'turn that bloody light off' and he'd been recycling old jokes for years.

He would have found the one about plastic bags taking a thousand years to decompose hilarious. Wait a minute, that's not a joke is it?

Once you've gone eco-friendly, you won't be alone. Everyone's getting into it now and with the excitement of different coloured bins, who can blame them? My neighbours are so enthusiastic about recycling glass that they're going through three of four bottles of wine a night.

Even God's doing his bit with the opening of some newly built Eco churches. I went to one which has solar panels on its roof and underfloor heating powered by thermal pipes, which are drilled one hundred metres into the earths core.

It means worshippers are being kept warm thanks to the burning fires of hell. You can guarantee most of the people down there were the type who used to leave their lights on.

*The Joy of Being Magical

T here was a time when magicians ruled the world. Not when Paul Daniels was on telly but in the days of Merlin. They all had white beards and cloaks back then and were renowned for that trick where they say, 'Is this your card?' and it isn't, and you think they're rubbish but then they put their hand in their cloak pocket and it's there instead!

In the dark ages, people thought wizards and sorcerers had supernatural powers and, as they were real sticklers for the only-doing-a-trick-once rule, it was no wonder.

These days, though, we're clever enough to realise that magic is all about illusion. Now you see it, now you don't. It's sleight of hand, showmanship and subtle distraction, but you won't get far without a wand and a magic word that actually works.

Most families contain someone who's known for having a few tricks up their sleeve. In ours its Uncle Magic Jimmy. His expertise has left Fitzpatrick children disappointed in many a professional party clown by comparison. They're

The Joy of Being Magical

mesmerised by his Peter and Paul disappearing bird finger trick and I must admit I'm still struggling to work it out myself. Peter's there, then Paul's there. Then Peter again so where's Paul gone? It's a relief when they both come back at the end.

When I was a kid he used to hold me up against the wall and say: 'Get out of that without moving!' And I couldn't! Escapology was never my forte.

His real speciality though is sawing people in two. He tends to work with his half-brother and his half-sister, but if anyone in the audience is half-cut he's happy to have a go on them as well.

More generally, women are well known for their magical powers, with most having a special knack for making coins disapear. Their next trick is usually pulling a new top out of a bag. And a surprising amount of men I know have a talent for vanishing when it's their round, only to miraculously reappear when someone else has got the drinks in.

For most magicians the pleasure is in seeing shock and awe in the faces of those they're entertaining, but some do earn lots of money at it. David Blaine managed to make a fortune appear in his bank account just by standing on top of a pole for two days. Now that really is magic.

The Joy of Being Rich

I t's not all it's cracked up to be, being rich, you know. I get up in a morning and have to walk half a mile, from my bedroom to my kitchen. Then I have to choose something from a big long list of fancy dishes for my chef to cook. I sometimes reminisce about the days when I had No Frills fruit and fibre. That stuff certainly keeps you regular.

Life's not always been like this, though. I often have to remind myself of where I came from. It was actually the west wing, seventh door on the left. Take a wrong turn on the way to breakfast and I could be lost for days.

Growing up, it was pretty tough in our house. We didn't have two pennies to rub together, which is what rich people spend most of their time doing. It was a rough area as well. My mum sent to the corner shop to get her some tights and they asked me what head size I wanted. She used to say to me: 'If you get murdered, I'll kill you!'

It was a worrying time but then, one day, I bought an apple for ten pence, shined it up and sold it for twenty. The day after I bought two apples, shined them up and sold

The Joy of Being Rich

them for forty. The day after that, some long lost aunt died and I inherited £40 million. That's capitalism for you, it rewards hard work and enterprise. Now I spend much of my time in helicopters and on yachts, or just lost in the west wing.

Turns out it's much more fun being loaded than being skint, especially when you've got more money than sense. It's a rich man's world, you see, and money makes it go round. People do say it's better to go to heaven in rags than hell in embroidery, but I'm guessing they've never worn a fifteen-thousand pound suit.

Some rich people get a bit obsessed by the material things though. A friend of mine crashed his car and sobbed: 'My Porsche, my Porsche!' The paramedic said: 'Forget your car, look at the state of your arm.' So then he said: 'My Rolex, my Rolex!'

If you have got lots of cash then it's a good idea to get an accountant and, luckily, my brother is a brilliant one. He told me there are just three kinds of accountants in this world, the ones who can count, and the ones who can't.

Mine is a story of rags to riches and you can do it to if you've got a burning desire to better yourself, or an auntie who gets hit by a truck. I'd say though that it's better to be poor and happy than rich and sad. Always remember that having money isn't everything, although it doesn't half keep the kids in touch.

*

The Joy of Sulking

As a general rule there are two kinds of sulks. Those that come on all of a sudden and begin with a dramatic crossing of arms or a big storm off, and those that arrive gradually as you mutter yourself into a stew.

However you come to begin sulking, at the moment you decide that's what you're going to do, you have to contort your face in a way which suggests you've just caught whiff of a particularly putrid smell.

It's entirely acceptable to establish your sulk where you are but storming off is by far the most attention grabbing route into a sulkathon. Within a couple of steps you should think about where you're heading. It has to be somewhere you can be found or there's no point. If you're too well hidden it'll be difficult for the person who's caused the huff to chase after you and beg your forgiveness with the grovelling apology you undoubtedly deserve.

A good rule of thumb is to find somewhere where they can see you but you can't see them. In bed fits the bill but if steep stairs are involved in your storm off it can be difficult to breath under the covers. To be found sulking in bed with your head visible and gasping for air will undermine your victim status.

A good place is under the coats if you're lucky enough to have some lined up on a row of hooks. Your top half should be well covered but your legs are visible and there's also a very good chance it's downstairs.

Spend the first few minutes of your sulk reinforcing your views about your victimisation. Imagine yourself forcefully explaining to the cause of your strop how hurt and upset you are and how next time their favourite programme is on telly you'll switch it over to see how they like it.

Traditional sulking involves cutting off your nose to spite your face. I'd suggest those who think it is a needlessly self-destructive over-reaction to a problem have obviously never emerged victorious after three days under the coats.

However determined to suffer you are, there will come a moment in every sulk when you have to decide it is time to come out of it. You can dismiss the possibility a couple of times by shaking your head and saying: 'No.' But unless you're going to sulk for the rest of your life it will eventually have to end.

If the sulk had a quick and extravagant entrance then it can be over just as quickly, but sulks that come on gradually may take years to disappear.

The worst thing you can do to someone in a sulk is accuse them of being childish. That will only make them dig their little heels in further. The best plan is to ignore them or make them laugh. If they're sulking over a misunderstanding then a little teasing could help, but if they've fallen out with you because you've just stolen their husband or wife, saying, 'Come on, silly…' might not do the trick.

*

The Joy of Driving

escribed affectionately as 'a two-ton killing machine', the car has made getting from A to B pretty easy. There's now no need to walk anywhere and there have been no greater advocates of the redundancy of legs than the parents of primary school children. The fact that it's helped us to grow a generation of chubby kids has got to be a bonus.

Driving is the process of getting your car to move and there's a whole range of styles you can adopt. The two styles at opposite ends of the spectrum are 'before your test' and 'after your test'. Then there's the 'boy racer' and 'the old woman' but I think the most enjoyable is 'the back seat driver'. You can actually adopt it wherever you're sitting as long as you're a passenger and in a patronising mood.

Before your test, you're required to hold the steering wheel with your hands at two o'clock and ten o'clock respectively. Post-test, the left hand should be at eleven o'clock and the right hand out of the window gesticulating at someone who's not going fast enough.

You need to learn your traffic signs. Red means stop,

The Joy of Driving

green means go and nobody really understands what amber means. Two fingers would suggest that you just cut someone up. Indicators are there to notify other motorists of intended turns but don't feel obliged to use them. You should also have a laid back approach to the idea of sticking to one lane at a roundabout.

Female drivers are known for their reverse parking prowess and mastery of the seventeen-point turn, while men insist on parking in ridiculously tight spaces just because they can.

Your attitude to driving will determine how much you enjoy it and if you think the world is against you it probably is. Lights will change and upset you, nobody will let you out no matter how angry you get and it will feel like the speed limits are there just to slow you down. I'd recommend trying to relax as you drive, but you should generally keep your eyes open.

Finally, let's talk about safety because accidents do happen. You'll find that in virtually every case it is someone else's fault. 'All of a sudden, a wall came out of nowhere.' Technology has moved on in motoring with air bags and a stronger car structure to protect you, but they've still not found a way of changing the nut at the wheel. Until that happens you might be better off walking. Unless you've got to go more than a hundred metres of course. Walking that far would just be ridiculous.

*

The Joy of Buffet Grazing

E very weekend the world plays host to millions of parties. And you know what that means. Millions of buffets. The first rule is always to get there first.

When the buffet starter pistol has been fired it's no time for politeness. That conversation with your uncle Geoff had outstayed its welcome anyway.

So, get to the front, legs about a shoulder's width apart and begin to scan. You're scanning for your make or break buffet ingredient and, for me, that means cocktail sausages. And not those hot dog ones on a stick with a pickled onion either, proper little sausages. On this alone, I can judge the buffet experience which lies ahead. If you're a veggie, you can apply the same rule with lettuce.

The queue is building behind you but thrive on that pressure. This is the reason you turned up tonight.

And you're off... ham sandwich, egg mayonnaise, tuna pasta... that'll do. Time to move on.

Cocktail sausages, I always have three, cheesy Wotsits, normal crisps... they're bound to be salt and vinegar.

The Joy of Buffet Grazing

You're freestyling, you're feeling it. This is a good buffet. Onion bhaji, spring roll... keep moving, keep breathing... tomato, cucumber, some sliced peppers to dip. Pizza, I can take it or leave it. Quiche, I'll take a slice but I won't eat it. Ah yes, three more cocktail sausages. Chocolate gateaux is to be collected on the second or third visit but, to be honest, if you need to know that then I'm wasting my time.

And there we have it. Find a seat, explain to my wife why I didn't get her anything, stop talking and get stuck in.

Now what I've described is the perfect buffet performance, but things can go disastrously wrong if you're not on the ball. At a Fitzpatrick christening a few years ago hesitation led to tragedy. By the time we got there, coleslaw and broken crisps were all that remained. Even the vegetable quiche had gone. What an experience like that does though is ensure the same mistake is never made again.

And the buffet world is changing. There are cold buffets, hot buffets and buffets with some hot bits and some cold bits. Sometimes there'll be prawns, sometimes there won't. But you'll never go wrong if you use cocktails sausages, proper ones, or lettuce, as your barometer.

Treat a buffet with respect but don't stand on ceremony. Graze as a cow in a field of lush grass but always be aware that there's a herd of angry lawn mowers hovering close behind.

*

The Joy of Being Sporty

The first thing you need if you're going to be sporty is a tracksuit. Shiny, if possible, and tucked into some football socks. This is what you have to wear all the time, especially for things like court appearances and funerals when you've no intention of playing any sport.

When the action starts though, it's time to reveal your serious attire. If you're a man, tight white shorts and white legs are the optimum outfit. Ideally, opponents should have to squint to see where the legs begin and the shorts end. Ladies, I suggest matching lycra leggings and T-shirt which also matches your baggy jumper and eye shadow.

So you've got the clothes, now you need a sport and you have the choice of team or individual. Being part of a team means you get to share the highs and lows. Individual means you get all the glory but can't blame humiliating defeats on anyone else.

You might decide to join a gym first to get fit. You'll spend your introductory session nodding intently at someone with a clipboard as they show you the settings on

The Joy of Being Sporty

an exercise bike and existing members mumble that you won't last long. Once settled you can attempt to bench press the weight of a small island or go to the 'Legs, Chins and Bingo Wings' class.

Running works out a bit cheaper than the gym because all you need is a road and some legs. If you're coordinated enough to do something with your hands at the same time you might like racquet sports. Squash, especially, is perfect if you enjoy getting sweat in your eyes.

Whatever team sport you play your aim should be not to get picked last. The only thing worse than that is the 'no, seriously, you have him, we'll play a man down' conversation. Other options are extreme sports like kite surfing and mother-in-law baiting. And it's worth noting that snooker and darts aren't sports, they're just excuses to go to the pub.

Rugby league is my chosen sport and, in my prime, I was known as a bit of a crowd-pleaser. When I had the ball you got the feeling that either team could score.

Sadly, for anyone sporty, age eventually catches up and I knew it was happening to me when a spectator enquired about my concrete boots. I can still change a game though. I recently went on as sub and it was nil-nil. Ten minutes later, we were eighteen-nil down.

For older sports enthusiasts, the best way to improve is to retire. Within a few weeks you'll be twice the player you used to be. Within a decade you will have been an absolute world beater with no equal in the modern game. It's something I'm having to consider.

✱

The Joy of Being Artistic

rt, much like beauty, is in the eye of the beholder. But artists, unlike beauticians, can claim that a shark filled with formaldehyde is a work of genius worth millions of pounds. Surprisingly though, there are still more people studying beauty therapy at college than art.

My uncle's an artist and a very good one too. You know he's good because it's impossible to work out the meaning of his creations without him explaining them. Of course, being an artist, this isn't something he's keen to do. 'What does it mean to you?' he'll say. I scream in exasperation: 'Is it or is it not a flippin' boat on a bit of water?' 'Hmm,' he replies. 'Interesting interpretation.'

It obviously runs in the family because the first thing I do in a morning is draw the curtains. I tend to work quite slowly which is why I've done numerous portraits of rotten fruit.

Feedback is never far away because my dad's a bit of an art expert. 'That's crap,' is his usual critique. It was quite hard to take as a seven-year-old, having spent hours making

The Joy of Being Artistic

a *papier maché* model of his head. He didn't even like the big ears.

But the approval of others isn't what's needed to make your art worthwhile. You're as unique as everyone else and what matters is that you express yourself. Whether you're sticking bits of dry pasta onto cardboard plates and covering them in glitter, or dipping potatoes in paint and pressing them onto paper, your work should be vehicle for you innermost thoughts and desires.

Abstract art is your best bet because the whole point is that it resembles nothing it's supposed to. If someone suggests your work looks like it was done by a five-year-old, then you'll know you're making progress.

A few arty facts for you…

1. Drawing with pencils and chalk is for people who are rubbish at painting.

2. Most people become artists so they can look at nude models.

3. Building a beach monster out of sand when you're on holiday doesn't mean you're a sculptor.

Once artistic I'm afraid it's unlikely you'll make a great deal of money until you're dead. In the meantime you can just force your family and people you know to put it on their walls. Be a bit concerned though if your doctor is mad keen to buy it all. He might know something you don't and that plaster of paris flower you made could be worth a fortune sooner than you think.

✳

The Joy of Cycling

T he impression you're likely to get from a book of old English clichés is that once you've learnt how to ride a bike, it will be easy for the rest of your life.

Well, it's a complete lie. When I got on a bike last year for the first time in a decade, this revelation only hit me as I edged over the top of a brow and began to descend down a steep hill with frightening ferocity.

I picked up speed as the wind whistled in my ears and my heart pounded a lot faster than I recollect it did when I was ten. A fly flew into one of my watery eyes as a bus thundered past within an inch of the end of my handlebars and, I can't be sure, but I may have let out a little squeal.

Thank God I'd still got the stabilisers on.

Terror aside though, I've since rediscovered cycling and found it's just about the most fun you can have on two wheels if you're not on a motorbike. Whether you are trundling along a canal towpath admiring the view or tearing down a dual carriageway because you missed the no bikes sign and need to get off, it can be a real pleasure.

The Joy of Being Cycling

It's always worth checking that everything's working and well oiled before you set off, legs being a priority, and I'd suggest you ensure your seat is at a comfortable height and the ting-a-ling bell is within reach.

Riding on a flat road is fairly easy but stony hills can be a challenge, especially if you've forgotten you're in twenty-first gear as you begin your ascent. Dropping to lower gears as you approach a hill will improve your chances of reaching the summit but my little tip would be to travel up in a car.

Cycling with a group can be really enjoyable and a good motivation to push yourself if they're a supportive bunch. I went with friends recently and fell so far behind they were convinced there was something wrong with my bike. I dismissed the suggestion but they insisted I get off so they could check it out.

All in all though, I've really enjoyed getting back in the saddle. Even on that first ride, after the near-death hill/fly/bus experience, I was feeling pretty confident by the time I'd gone round the village.

I remember turning round to my dad who looked overwhelmed with pride and mud thrown up by the back tyre. I said: 'You can let go of the seat now. I think I've got my balance.'

*

The Joy of Kite Flying

I don't care what your doctor says, if you've got wind, I'd recommend you get yourself a kite. Just go out into the open air and let one go and I guarantee you'll feel much better. It's one of the most natural things you can do and I don't mind admitting I find it pretty enjoyable.

In the good old days when people used to make their own kites, all you needed was a bit of tissue paper and a couple of sticks. But modern kites actually fly.

The traditional shape is still a diamond with a little tail and a bow but now you can buy almost any shape and style you want. And there's no shortage of wind about either.

Most famous is the silent but deadly brand, renowned for sneaking up unexpectedly and hitting people in the face. There are noisy, hurricane-like gusts which can come as a shock to everybody.

And then there's wind that lingers in a persistent, unforgiving manner. With a modern kite, this will do fine because what you're after is a smooth, steady breeze.

The Joy of Kite Flying

Whatever kind of wind you're dealing with, the point of release is crucial. I'd recommend you do it in a location where you have enough room to run. This means confined spaces with lots of people aren't ideal, although some people are happy to have a go wherever they are.

Generally, though, you should find a wide open space and get a glamorous assistant to hold your kite up for you. They have to really stretch, like they want to ask a question at primary school. Let a bit of line out and then wait for some wind. It may take you by surprise but it's likely you'll sense its coming.

And you're off! Let the kite fly away from you a little, then pull in on the line, let it out and pull it in again until it climbs up and up to the highest height, dancing majestically across the sky as it tussles with a temperamental and teasing force of nature. Awesome.

My favourite place to fly kites is at the beach. When there's miles of open sand and a strong and true sea breeze, you really can't go wrong. Unless you happen to leave your little cousin in charge of a six-foot stunt kite shaped like a dragon.

I have to say the coastguards were very understanding when they picked him up somewhere near the Shetland Isles. The first thing he said when he was back on dry land was: 'I won't be eating that again.'

*

The Joy of Gardening

I t used to be thought that you needed green fingers to be good at gardening. Then someone realised that the pesticides turning them green probably weren't good for your vegetables. Yes, you had nurtured a ridiculously big courgette but, really, who wants fingers like that?

For those who enjoy gardening, there are few things more satisfying. It should be done in spurts with a smile. A trim of a rose bush here, a removal of weed there, a paving over of a large area of grass because cutting it takes too much effort, over yonder. There's a time to plant and a time to prune but, most importantly, a time to sit back and appreciate your own handiwork.

Once you've got a garden or allotment, all you need is some ready made hanging baskets from the garden centre. For your beds you've got perennials, annuals (*Girls Aloud 2010* is brilliant) and biennials. Bulbs can add colour but the environmentally friendly ones do take ages to blossom.

Lots of people are now growing their own vegetables

The Joy of Gardening

and if you get good manure you can really taste it. It's much more satisfying than buying veg from a supermarket but I do think it's a pity it doesn't come out washed, sliced and vacuum-packed.

Osteopaths are particularly keen on gardening. They don't do it themselves but they make a fortune from those who thought they'd 'just turn that flower bed over'. My grandad had a neat little trick to protect his back, which was to get me to do it.

Expert help is available on every street in the UK if you need it. I get mine from Keith next door. A while ago he said: 'Isn't it time you sorted out that rainforest you call a lawn?' I took his advice and a found a soggy old tennis ball within minutes, which was an unexpected bonus.

The sworn enemies of gardeners are slugs and snails. If B&Q sold infra-red pellet guns they'd do a roaring trade and exhausted gardeners would not be up all night at their bedroom window scanning their begonias.

Finally, if you want to mix things up you could always try naked gardening, which is becoming increasingly popular in areas where they can't get Channel Five. I considered mowing the lawn in the nude recently and asked my wife what the neighbours might think. She said: 'They'll probably think I married you for your money.'

*
The Joy of Photography

When photography first became popular in the mid-1800s, it must have left people in awe. The idea that their image could be frozen in time and held for posterity would have been wondrous. If only they could see some of the pictures people put on Facebook now.

Back then, you'd be lucky and wealthy if you appeared in one family photograph. Today you can feature in forty on a night out.

You need a good eye to take a decent photo and it's even better if you've got two. The secret is in the framing, whether it's the dog in a silly hat or a cherry tree resplendent in full bloom.

I advise you make a square with your thumbs and fore fingers, then close one eye and look through the square while moving it forwards and back. Once you've located your shot, alternate your eyes a couple of times and you are ready for action.

If photographing people, it's now time to get your

The Joy of Photography

subject to pose. I'm a traditionalist so I recommend: 'Say cheese!' Anything else is just a cheap imitation. Start clicking the button and let your artistic juices flow. Work it baby, work it. That's it, talk to me, through the camera.

In the days of film you wouldn't know what you'd taken until it had been developed. After hours in a darkened room with negatives, pegs and washing lines, it could be a disappointment to find that you'd cut the top off the tree and the dog was looking at the telly instead of you. Sometimes I'd come back into the light after a few hours and my wife would say: 'Why the long lens?'

But digital cameras have led to a revolution in photography. Even complete amateurs can now manage to get superb shots of the back of their children's heads. Also, while red eye used to be something of a rarity, it is now possible on virtually every photograph.

Getting shots of things that move can be a particular challenge on digital cameras. We were at a fair the other week and some poor child spent three quarters of an hour on the waltzer as his Dad attempted to get a shot of him waving. He failed but he did manage to get forty-two crackers of the lad being sick afterwards.

One thing technology hasn't done is make posing for photos in family groups any easier, especially if one of your parents is in charge of their new camera. 'Here we go... no, wait a minute. Keep posing, keep posing. Did it flash?'

The reply comes in unison. 'No Dad. You haven't switched it on.' I bet that happened in the 1800s as well.

*

The Joy of Swimming

I t is a well known fact that if you're on a boat and it sinks, you've got a better chance of survival if it's three in the morning on a fairly chilly night. This is because it's very likely you'll be wearing pyjamas. If you've got a brick handy as well, the likelihood of you making it to shore increases yet further.

Understandable, then, that treading water in pyjamas is the foundation on which our nation's swimming capability is built.

Most people start splashing around as babies or toddlers before signing up for lessons where there's a whole host of different metre length challenges lined up for you. At no other time in your life will you try so hard to win a fabric badge.

Swimming teachers have different styles. One at the pool I learnt at used to chuck his pupils in on their first lesson is a display of tough love. A couple drowned but, on the whole, his approach created a generation of strong swimmers in tears.

The Joy of Swimming

Once you've got your ten metres and don't sink very often you can begin to learn different strokes and choose one which suits you best. They all involve moving your arms and legs about to propel you through the water.

Breast stroke is the most popular which is surprising with all the no heavy petting signs. Front crawl is the fastest but it isn't ideal if you're wearing glasses. My favourite is back crawl, but I wouldn't recommend it if you've got crippling paranoia. Butterfly is for real show-offs who are trying to prove something, but you can never be sure they're actually doing it anyway because there's so much splashing.

Early each morning our public pools are full of people trying to swim in a straight line. Some regulars like to use the same lane every day and woe betide anyone who backstrokes across it. The old ladies especially get really shirty if you dive bomb in the shallow end as they approach.

If you don't swim regularly though, foreign holidays are where you're most likely to get in a pool and have some fun. However hot it is outside, you should never underestimate how cold the water will be. Counting to three is the best way to convince yourself to jump in. If you get to twenty, it's probably best to return to your book.

*

The Joy of Jigsawing

N othing says 'retirement home' quite like a wooden board and a half-done jigsaw. Cast among the old dears, pot plants and custard creams, you can't help but wonder if it will ever get finished.

That, after all, is a jigsaw's destiny and it's a responsibility jigsawers shouldn't take lightly. To you, clipping individual pieces into place may just seem like an crazy, adrenaline-filled night in but, to the jigsaw, it could be its one chance to ever feel complete.

And they take rejection hard, a bit like a man when he's had a drink and misread the signs before sauntering upstairs to find his wife is actually tucked up in bed in her comfy pyjamas. If you think that's disappointing, imagine how a jigsaw feels when someone puts a couple of edge pieces together and then decides they'd rather go and make some cheese on toast.

You should only embark upon a jigsaw if you're committed to seeing it though. No-one is saying a three-

The Joy of Jigsawing

thousand piece autumn forest scene is easy, it's not supposed to be, but getting to the end will make it all worthwhile. If footloose and fancy free is more your style, you'd be better suited to Scrabble.

Set your stall out so you've got plenty of room and no disturbances. Perhaps put *Countdown* on in the background to create the right ambience. I like to have a lukewarm cup of tea nearby for refuelling.

Spread the jigsaw out on a solid and supportive surface (we'll find out why later) and begin flipping the pieces over so the picture is facing up. Find the corners (there should be four of those) and separate the edge pieces from those with character on all sides.

You then begin methodically, first completing the outer edge before working your way towards the middle. You may, on occasion, take time out to work on a particularly identifiable central section but don't allow yourself to become too frequently distracted or you'll lose momentum. Dedication and patience are vital but what you really need for success is a lump hammer.

Obviously you should begin any jigsaw fully intending to get every piece in the correct place but when that's not working, it is acceptable practice to 'encourage' them to fit. I usually persuade any spare pieces to take up residence in the empty spaces and then touch them up with a bit of poster paint. All the jigsaw masters do it.

Whether it's a five-piece Peppa Pig jigsaw or a two-thousand piece portrait of the Queen, the moment when you hammer in the final piece and sit back to admire your efforts is pretty special. And there's only one way to celebrate. How else, but with a party popper and a Werther's Original?

Around the House

*

The Joy of Brewing Up

O n average the British drink three cups of tea a day. That's six brews every two days and so on until, after a couple of weeks, we really have drunk quite a few. It's been like this since the 1500s, when tea leaves arrived here from India. Since then, tea has been the antidote to all known disasters.

It is most commonly used as a sedative to help cope with bad news. 'Gordon, I'm afraid the world appears to have been destroyed by an asteroid. Don't worry though, I'll put the kettle on and we'll have nice cup of tea.' It is essential that the tea you have in these situations is 'nice' or it won't solve anything. This means its important to know how people like their brew.

If someone drinks Builders Tea Two and you give them Watery Milk One they won't be impressed. If Gordon says: 'Just threaten it with a tea bag' and you forget about the bag and then burst it when retrieving it, he might actually realise the end of the world is quite upsetting.

Generally, the best way to brew up is in a warm teapot

103

The Joy of Brewing Up

while listening to big band music, but single cup brewing is more common and it should be taken no less seriously. A desire for perfection is essential. Drop the bag, pour boiling water, stir once then leave for a period determined by the desired strength and remember, seconds count. Gently squeeze then remove the bag. Add milk, stir again, sip and sigh.

Sugar is necessary for anyone who's not quite sweet enough. Some people have a spoon and a quarter, some have three. Some people just put a drop of tea in the sugar bowl and drink it through a straw.

In recent years new designs of tea bags have come onto the market to shake things up a bit. With round ones and those shaped as pyramids the theory is that given greater room to move within the bag, the leaves will release more flavour into your brew. They're scientifically proven to work better as a marketing tool than the ordinary ones.

You shouldn't just restrict yourself to ordinary tea when brewing. Peppermint tea is good for digestion. Camomile is said to be soothing. Raspberry can kick-start labour. Earl Grey is also popular, especially with Communists, who believe that all proper tea is theft.

However skilled you are at brewing up though, it's always nicer to drink a cup of tea made by someone else. 'Do you fancy a brew?' I tend to say to my wife. 'Great. Then I'll have one with you.'

The Joy of Biscuit Dipping

People of a carefree nature will say it's just the way the cookie crumbles but, really, it all depends on how long you leave your biscuit in your brew. Biscuit dipping is one of those wonderful skills in life which everyone can possess, if only they put in the practice.

First though, let's make one thing clear; not everyone is a fan of biscuit dipping. In fact, in some places it's positively frowned upon. Like the fancy hotel I once visited. The owner's jaw dropped when he noticed me mid-dip with one of his homemade shortbreads. His face scrunched with horror as I bit into the biscuit and half of it broke off and tumbled, in slow motion, into the cup of tea below.

I smiled proudly. Sometimes biscuit dippers have to hold their nerve in the face of adversity. At other times cunning and guile is needed. My grandad always said: 'Eh, what are your teeth for?' It meant I had to distract him and dip when he wasn't looking.

Obviously, you need a cup of tea or coffee, then you need a biscuit and the barrel of choice runs pretty deep. Long thin

The Joy of Biscuit Dipping

ones, short thick ones, long thick ones, short thin ones. Round ones, square ones, chocolate ones and ones with jam in. Set yourself with a firm grip, assess the biscuit's size, shape and thickness and remember less is more, speed and style is everything.

The crucial point isn't, as a novice may suggest, the moment when you dip. It's the moment when you withdraw. A second too soon and there'll be a lingering crunch in the centre, which is frankly unacceptable. A second too late and you'll have to teaspoon the biscuit out. Unmitigated disaster.

Knowing when to retreat is partly visual, partly instinct but massively important is technique. Trust your senses then withdraw, gracefully swinging your hand downwards, leaving the biscuit in a vertical position, the un-dipped base providing support for the section weakened by moisture.

There's no time to admire your handiwork. Retreat and eat. If need be return for a second dip, but two dips per biscuit is the standard I'd expect. Challenge yourself and push the boundaries. Vary the biscuits you dip but be aware of the risks as well as the rewards.

It's also essential you appreciate the difference between dipping and dunking. In my view dunking is for clumsy amateurs, dipping is for the connoisseur. Dip with passion, dip with pride. Dip in public, you've nothing to hide.

*

The Joy of DIY

I t's not as easy as you might think to earn the title of DIY expert. Anyone can describe themselves in that way but the real challenge is to have people convinced that you know what you're doing with a hammer and a packet of screws.

First up, you'll need a large tool box and carefully planned contents. Get everything you need but more importantly, get the tools that you don't need, the one's only a real tradesman would have. Things like a full spanner set, a wood plane, lots of metal washers and a tiny little paint brush which is neither use nor ornament. You want to give the impression that you're anything but a cowboy. You might work in an office or cut hair for a living but your real calling, your vocation in life, is working miracles with your hands and the tool set you got for Christmas.

Making people think you're an expert is more important than whether you can actually put up a set of shelves and get them to be that level thing. What you need is evidence of your expertise and people should be reminded of it at every opportunity. After I split my front bedroom into two anyone who visited the house was given the tour. I'd say: 'I know what you're thinking, a team of craftsmen must have worked on this.' Their nods of agreement quickly turned to shock as I explain that actually I did it all myself. And my dad helped a bit.

Never let an opportunity to claim you know what you're talking about slip through your fingers, wherever you are. Point out sloppy workmanship at other people's houses and suggest they should have asked you to do it. Make use of the disappointed sigh whenever you're talking about a potential job, always over emphasise how difficult it will be and then reassure the customer, your mum or whoever, that it's well within your capabilities and level of skill. I tend to do that even when I'm weighing a job up on my own and there's no-one there. Practice makes perfect.

When you buy bits of gear from the DIY shop, wood, Polyfilla or coat hooks, always get more than you need. The more you buy, the more jobs you must have on, the more likely they'll believe you're a DIY expert.

Be careful not to get carried away by your own publicity though. When I asked for discount at my local hardware shop in exchange for a life-size cut-out of myself wearing a tool belt and saying 'I shop here', they weren't bowled over by the idea. 'A bit like the Ronseal man,' I explained. They decided to think about it and in the meantime I had to pay full price for forty light bulbs, some masking tape and a thousand four-inch nails.

You need a special mug. Mine says 'DIY Superstar'. And one final tip, it's always a good idea to have your phone handy and the number of someone who actually knows what they're doing.

*

The Joy of Camping

When those who camp reflect on another classic British summertime, it is almost certainly memories of nights spent shivering in a tent that will make them smile most. After all, camping is as big a passion in this country as moaning about the shocking weather.

Camping traditionalists will say all you need to get started is a tent, a sleeping bag and a mat. But essentials I'd also recommend are a little stove which takes forever to heat anything, some insect repellent and a torch. The importance of the latter was rammed home by a couple I interrupted when climbing into the wrong tent on the way back from a 4am toilet visit.

These days, tents are refreshingly easy to put up, but most still don't have a telly. Long poles arc up to raise the roof and you can erect an enormous five-bedroom mansion with a kitchen and dining area in no time. Where there used to be twenty tents in a field there are now just three. I've even got one friend who bragged he'd found a tent with a

The Joy of Camping

tiled floor but, on reading the small print, it turned out he'd bought a time-share in Marbella.

There's huge variety in the kind of campsite you can pitch up at. At one extreme you'll be alone in a field of long grass with a cold tap your only facility. At the other you'll be on a big commercial site where there are hot showers, entertainment and fields jam-packed with people who like to swear at their kids. I prefer a site somewhere in the middle with the cold tap and the swearing.

The real charm of camping is that you're so close to mother nature. Just a thin slightly waterproof material separates you and the big wide world. After a day spent enjoying the great outdoors and tiring the kids out, you can spend your evening being eaten alive as you relax with a glass of your favourite tipple in the open air.

Then it's bed time or 'bad back time' as you'll come to know it. 'We definitely need a blow-up bed,' is an oft-heard phrase among virgin campers, usually mumbled regrettably in a morning while their eyes are still stuck together. You'll also arise with a new-found respect for the all-conquering power of gravity, having awoken wedged up against a corner of the tent after pitching it on a slight hill.

But flick the sleep from your eyes, unzip the canvas and breath in that lovely fresh rain as another day of your holiday begins.

When the kettle finally boils in forty-five minutes time, it will be a cup of tea to savour. And that's the secret to enjoying camping. Savouring every bit of that difference to home. Otherwise all the suffering just isn't worthwhile.

*

The Joy of Building A Sandcastle

For a family man, a trip to the beach always ends in sacrifice. All he really wants to do is lie back, relax and top up his tan, but he can't help feeling obliged to get up and build a sandcastle.

It's for the kids, of course. And even though mine are too young to be interested for more than two minutes, I can't help feeling I'd be letting them down if I didn't step up and wrestle the spade off them.

It's a test of your prowess as a man in full view of your loved ones, other fathers, other children and women other than your wife, which is why I suggest keeping your chest tensed throughout the building process.

Make sure you're in the right area of the beach. Too close to the water and the sand will be soggy. Too far away and it will be too dry and crumbly. Importantly, though, you need to be close enough to the sea for it to fill your moat, because you can't set off home until it does.

Don't worry if you haven't got an architect-designed

The Joy of Building A Sandcastle

plan or any proper tools. The whole point really is that you battle on with the bucket and spade your little girl uses, but I did once spot a competitive Dad with a JCB on a beach in Cornwall.

I begin by drawing the shape of my intended castle. Then I dig the moat and throw the sand into the main building area. Dig, throw and pat. Dig, throw and pat. You'll soon get into a rhythm and, after a few hours, the base structure should be complete.

From here you begin filling buckets and covering your creation in turrets. Forty will be enough. Finally, a few shells the kids have collected should take pride of place at the top of your castle.

Loudly announce that: 'It'd take a tsunami to get rid of that' before you sit down, and prepare to convince doubting passers-by that you did actually build it by yourself, all on your own, with that little pink spade.

The moment the water drops into the six by six-inch channel you've cut and completes a circle around your masterpiece, it's time to pack up. Your work is done.

As you leave the beach, it is traditional to turn and savour one final, lingering look. I also tend to have a last thought and it's always the same. 'I'm definitely going to bring some scaffolding next time.'

*

The Joy of Having a Fire

The ability to harness fire is one the things which separates humans from the rest of the animal kingdom.

Apes, for example, may resemble us when they eat bananas or affectionately pick flies off each other's backs, but can you imagine them making a pretend body out of some trousers and a shirt and stuffing it with newspaper, before watching it burn as they pick treacle toffee out of their teeth? Probably not.

And yet, when you gaze into the dancing flames of a fierce blaze, there's an undeniable connection with our evolutionary forefathers. It's as if, in that moment, you're having exactly the same life experience as someone who lived hundreds of thousands of years ago. I think this hits home particularly with those new flat screen electric fires, where you're basically watching pornography for arsonists on a telly.

The main point of a fire is to create warmth and it's for those occasions when two jumpers just aren't enough.

The Joy of Having a Fire

Crucial elements are air, heat and fuel. If any one of these is missing then your fire will go out. Start by lighting tinder (paper/dry grass), then add kindling (small twigs) and finally chuck on fuel (wood/coal). For ignition, I'd always recommend matches but, if you're out in the wilderness with only your instincts, petrol and a self-lighting blowtorch, you'll just have to muddle through.

While having a 'real' fire in your own home is great, outdoor fires are where it's really at. It's wonderful to sit around a campfire with your friends and realise that none of you actually know any ghost stories. You can also do the Mexican wave continuously in a forlorn attempt to avoid getting smoke in your eyes.

Big public bonfires are one of the few remaining events where whole communities come together. Some of them are enormous and need a rope strung around to stop people getting so close that their faces melt. Smoking eyelashes are a sign that you should move, once you've finished your meat and potato pie.

While the big fire is exciting, it's likely another highlight of your evening will be the fireworks display. No matter how many of these you have seen before, it's still hard not to be impressed. You often hear people saying things like, 'Oooooooh', 'Ahhhh', 'Oooh', 'Ah', 'Shall we get a drink?'

✳
The Joy of Being Festive

I t's the most won-der-ful time... of the year! Jingle belling all the way, warming chestnuts slightly on a radiator and wearing a tinsel headband. Eating stale mince pies, kissing people under the mistletoe and getting a written warning for sexual harassment at the works do. Why can't the whole year be as much fun as this?

Christmas is about spending time with your family, seeing joy in the faces of young children and falling out over the rules of a new board game. Being festive is the only way you can survive it with a smile.

First job is to get a tree. There's great debate about real versus fake and there will never be agreement. I think they're all lovely but would say you only have to look at Jordan to see how things can get out of hand. Generally, flashing is frowned upon in this country but at Christmas it's essential. We have lights on our tree, our fireplace, front and back windows, in the porch and around the toilet bowl, understatement adding a touch of class.

Hopefully Santa will come and all the threats you made

The Joy of Being Festive

to your children about their behaviour will be vindicated. I recommend the frantic emptying of your stocking to remove oranges, apples and bits of coal (that's for older readers) so you can see if the big man has delivered what you ordered. Once said item has been located, I suggest you savour every tear, rip and revelation until… 'Oh, right. Did I ask for an ice scraper?'

At dinner, the turkey gets stuffed. Then so does everyone else. Christmas is not a great time for turkeys really, but it's their own fault for voting for it. All the trimmings should be there and if you're being festive then you've got to have a bit of everything. As my mum always says: 'Grandma didn't like sprouts and she ate them at Christmas so you can too.'

When pulling crackers it's about the winning not the taking part. Dads have to wear their paper hat in a way that makes everyone else want to adjust it and they'll read the jokes with unbridled enthusiasm. Then, as the evening progresses, you can treat yourself to a bit of indigestion as you look forward to turkey sandwiches, turkey salad and turkey soup in the days ahead.

The children should be worn out by now so you can settle down to watch someone die in *EastEnders*. Despite being mesmerised by the magic and the make-believe, kids are still astute enough not to miss a thing. 'You got lots of socks, dadda. You must have been a really naughty boy.'

It's just the most won-der-ful time of the year.

*

The Joy of New Years Resolutions

The start of a new year is a time of hope, excitement and sobering up. It's the day after the night before and the day before the night after which, if you've set a new years resolution, is when you're probably thinking about giving it up.

The dawning of a new year is a fresh start, a rare moment of opportunity. Last year may have been disastrous but don't be disheartened. In the new one there'll be boundless opportunities for fresh disasters. Just think of the things you might not achieve in the next twelve months? The list is almost endless.

Failing to stick to resolutions is part of our culture. We're even gallant losers when competing with our own mind. But if you get past dinnertime on day one, you're heading into day two, just twenty-four hours away from day three. Day two hundred and sixty-five is almost within touching distance.

It's important that your resolution is achievable. 'Marry Brad Pitt' is one which has been popular with women over the years and in every case but two it has led to bitter

The Joy of New Years Resolutions

disappointment. The general areas people focus on are health, well-being and wealth, with the usual suspects of giving up smoking, joining a gym, spending more time with the family and winning the lottery.

Stopping smoking is a tough one because if you've sailed this far through the rough waters of pubic vilification, there's a good chance that you actually enjoy it. Joining a gym is something new year resolutioners do in their droves, and they are usually found watching telly over the shoulder of the instructor doing their induction.

Spending more time with family is a heartfelt resolution and it's understandable that busy people yearn to be closer to those they love. There are of course some families who resolute to have more time away from each other, still traumatised by the Bank Holiday they spent stuck in a traffic jam on the M6.

If you're single then you may determine to find yourself a new partner. The best way to succeed with this resolution is to drop your standards. Do they have to be attractive and interesting? Why not aim for 'has a pulse' then anything else is a bonus.

If your resolution survives until February you've done very well indeed. You'll be looking better, feeling better and struggling to contain your smugness. If you've forgotten your resolution by the time you wake up on Thursday it's likely you're in the majority. But for a few minutes on New Years Eve it's nice to imagine we have the capacity to improve, isn't it?

And Finally...

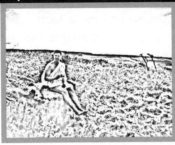

*

The Joy of Being a Local Celebrity

I never wanted any of this. It was just supposed to be a few hints and tips about essential skills in life but, before I knew it, I was getting recognised in the Co-op.

Turns out she thought I was someone else but it still goes on the list which, by the way, is approaching double figures.

Most people imagine it must be great to be a local celebrity, but there is a price to pay. Strangers approach me in the street and ask for the time or directions. Friends no longer invite me to parties under this bizarre pretence that 'I'm boring'.

Generally, there are two kinds of celebrities. Those who desire it and those who have it thrust upon them. Having it thrust upon you isn't particularly nice and, depending what it is, can be pretty unpleasant. But if you're keen on the idea of superstardom then you had better get yourself an agent.

I rang a few but they didn't get back. In the end I had to sanction some PR manoeuvres myself, like getting KEVIN sprayed on the sides of my tiger skin car. These days when people wonder 'who's that idiot?' there can be little doubt.

The Joy of Being a Local Celebrity

You can of course become a local celebrity for all the wrong reasons; if you're, perhaps, the local tramp who wanders the streets in an army jacket. Everyone knows what you look like and that you're usually carrying a plastic bag but, beyond that, you're shrouded in mystery. And muck. Or perhaps you got caught in a very public and compromising position and, before you know it, old ladies wink at you as they drive by on their mobility scooters. If only they'd let me explain.

Sometimes it's hard to gauge whether the public are star struck or just don't know me yet. Many still feign ignorance when I assure them I'm just a normal person as I point at my 'Learn with Kev' baseball cap.

Then there are the photographs. The other day a couple came up and asked if I'd mind taking a picture. 'Of course,' I said. 'Stand on my left and I'll try to look ironic.' Turned out they wanted me to take a photo of them! I kid you not.

It goes without saying that you'll need a fan club. My sister runs mine and a couple of bills have already arrived. I try to set aside time to read them all and would have written back, but I couldn't really understand the point they were making.

Finally, it's important for any celeb to have someone close who'll keep their feet on the ground. The other week I said to my wife, 'Eh, I got recognised again today!' She said, 'Who by, your dad?' A comment like that takes the wind out of your sails and reminds you that you're still only human, albeit with a particularly familiar face.

*

The Joy of Growing Old

My grandad used to say: 'There's nowt down for this growing old.' And he was right. I hit the big three-one a few (nine) months ago and all of a sudden the words hip hop had a new meaning.

I suppose it's easy for fairly young pups like myself to get a bit dramatic about it all. 'It could be worse,' suggested my smug, younger wife. 'You could be dead.' She then moved the hand holding my pipe off my knee and patted my corduroys.

Since then though, I've attempted to focus on the positives of getting older. After all, with age comes wisdom, a sense of one's true self and arthritis. You've seen it, done it and can't remember most of it.

Plus, age doesn't pigeon-hole you like it used to. The fifties are the new thirties and forty-six is the new twenty-two. That's mainly because so many people are divorced that everyone's back out on the pull with lower standards than the first time round.

You can work till you're seventy now and it's likely

The Joy of Growing Old

you'll have to. If you think nobody's interested in you in your twilight years, just try missing a couple of mortgage payments.

Once you eventually retire you can spend your time sat on benches watching pigeons argue, or have tea and scones at garden centres every day. Probably best to avoid the water features section afterwards.

The older you get the more stubborn and set in your ways you're allowed to become. My uncle Ralph always refused to budge whatever the situation. In fact, his dying words were: 'I'm not dipping my lights till he dips his.'

They say you should aim to live long enough to become a burden to your kids. Payback time has finally arrived! But do remember it's them who'll choose your care home.

Sadly, and inevitably, a consequence of growing old is that one day the end will come. Good health is merely the slowest possible rate at which you can die.

But after a life well lived you shouldn't be afraid. A great aunt of mine, for example, just lay back in a comfy chair and gently slipped into everlasting sleep. What a lovely way to go. It was a bit traumatic for the dentist though.

＊

The Joy of Social Networking

J ust because I look at home standing on a rock wrapped in a bed sheet, doesn't mean I'm not at the forefront when it comes to living in the modern world.

I'm on Facebook and Twitter and I'm thinking about getting one of those phones that you can walk around with. Go to 'learnwithkev' on Facebook and I'll send you a new skill guide every couple of weeks.

People keep telling me they're really excited when they think they've got a new message, but they then realise it's just a breathtakingly astute analysis of an essential activity from me. Gutted. I sense I'm being blamed for the fact that no-one else ever messages them.

These will be the same people who were a bit picky about the friends requests they accepted in the early days, but soon started accepting everyone when requests from people they actually knew or could remember dried up.

If you're really cool, though, you should get on Twitter. OMG! It's hard not to feel young and smug when you speak to someone who's not on there.

The Joy of Social Networking

'What do you write?' they say. 'Nothing, really,' I have to admit. 'You should have a go. You'd love it grandad.'

What you're aiming for on Twitter is to have more people following you than you follow, which takes some doing unless you start deleting people you follow once you've got them to follow you back.

The goal is to be following about 36 people, Stephen Fry among them, and have twelve thousand hanging on your every word. That's my plan anyway. If you go to 'learnwithkev' on Twitter you'll see that my subject to stalker ratio needs a little work.

Social networking has undoubtedly changed our lives forever. To have a real-time connection - albeit just 140 characters long - with random people you'll never properly know or meet around the world is surely an astonishing leap forward for human kind.

I for one think it beats having friends in your real life. Follow me and I'll follow you. I promise...

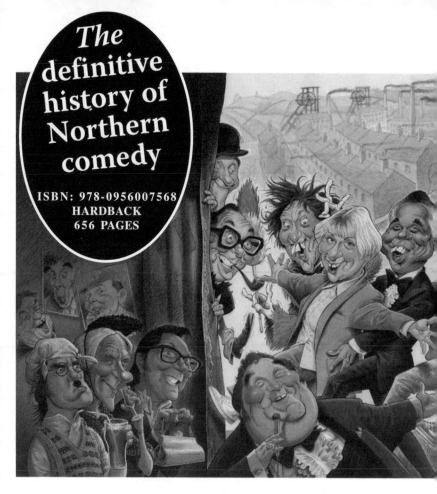

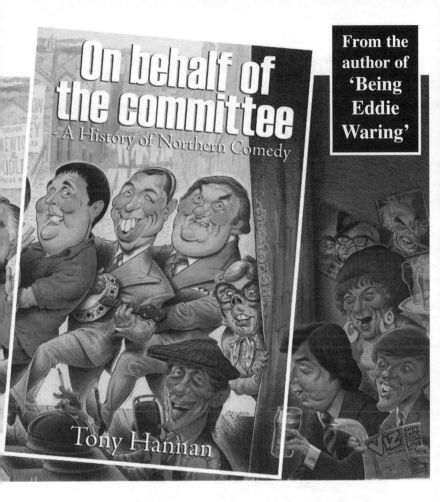

From the Industrial Revolution to our own 21st century digital age - via music hall, Variety, working mens clubs, radio, cinema & television - Northern-born comedians have been at the heart of popular British comedy culture.

This witty and informative book wonders why that should be so, and charts a course through the careers of George Formby, Tommy Handley, Gracie Fields, Frank Randle, Al Read, Jimmy James, Hylda Baker, Jimmy Clitheroe, Les Dawson, Morecambe & Wise, Bernard Manning, Victoria Wood, Ken Dodd, Vic and Bob, Steve Coogan, Caroline Aherne, the League of Gentlemen, Johnny Vegas, Peter Kay and many many others. Along the way, it also asks why that contribution should so often be under-appreciated.

Mostly, however, **On Behalf of the Committee** is a rich celebration of British comedy history, confirming that you really do have to laugh, or else you'd cry...